CALLED TO Serve

Rising to the Call

MARTI SZOSTAK

STRATTON
—P R E S S—
Publishing Life

CALLED TO SERVE
Copyright © 2018 **Marti Szostak**

Stratton Press, LLC
1603 Capitol Ave, Suite 310,
Cheyenne, WY 82001
www.stratton-press.com
1-888-323-7009

Because of the dynamic nature of the Internet, any web addresses or links contained in this book may have changed since publication and may no longer be valid. The views expressed in the work are solely those of the author and do not necessarily reflect the views of the publisher, and the publisher hereby disclaims any responsibility for them.

ISBN (Paperback): 978-1-64345-043-8
ISBN (Ebook): 978-1-64345-236-4

Printed in the United States of America

Introduction

People are like concrete—there is really only a very short time early in our lives when we can be molded before hardening. So many of us describe ourselves as *cradle Christians* who were taught as children to love and serve our God, and then went on our merry way becoming adults who gradually decided that we no longer needed our God, we no longer needed all those things we were taught as children about going to church and serving others, and we could make it on our own just fine. Although we left home prepared with lots of parental advice about the matter and lots of prayers by our parents, we slowly started chipping away at our concrete and became more and more streetwise, figuring out relatively quickly that we did not need to be there for others. It was *us* that we needed to be there for, it was *us* that we were trying to make rich, and it was *us* that we needed to take care of. Our parents were old and some of them were even zealots. They didn't really know what makes a person happy and what a young person needs. They could get by with being somewhat poor and didn't mind that. Parents don't really know what the young people of today need. Many parents just pray fervently for their children that they will be led by the spirit to do good and serve others, and many of their children leave home patronizing their parents' advice and prayers with little intent on following their advice or needing their prayers.

It seems that many of us today are kind of in a state of spiritual drowsiness with widespread indifference. Many so-called Christians have settled into a state of *insensate lethargy* as to what they should be doing for others. They are like the foolish virgins of the Bible who fell asleep while the bridegroom was delayed, and then slept right through it when the bridegroom did come; or like Jonah, who was fast asleep in the boat while the storms raged and then was finally swept into the seas. To many, this translates into an unresponsiveness to the call of God. It is high time that these Christians awaken from their slumber. St. Paul told the people of Ephesus to "Awake, you who sleep, arise from the dead and Christ will give you light" (Eph. 5:14).

We must change our world from one of "me, me, me" and do so with an unselfish and giving heart. We were made for our God to use us as *He* sees fit—for *His* purposes and not for our own. We must close the abyss between what we say and how we live. We must show our quiet wisdom and unfaltering faith in all that we do, and we must become an inspiration to those whose paths we cross, shining through our gentle love on earth. We must strive to always have a compassionate and loving heart that will change the world around us a little bit each day with every small loving act that we do. We should try to recognize that every day brings us a chance to be holy like we have always wanted to be, a chance to be someone we could not be yesterday as we were too focused on ourselves. Our motto must be that we be remembered and recognized as a slave of Jesus Christ!

Through this book, it is my hope and prayer that I may speak through the mouth of the Holy Spirit all that He wishes me to say; and that those who read my words may hear them through the ears of God and see them through the eyes of God. And may that, in turn, spur you on to become true servants of Christ who answer the call to serve. "But

Jesus called them to Him and said…'Anyone who wants to become great among you must be your servant, and anyone who wants to be first among you must be your slave, just as the Son of man came not to be served but to serve, and to give his life as a ransom for many'" (Matt. 20:24–28).

God, You have loved me from the
moment of my creation.
You've forgiven me for the things I
believed were unforgivable.
You've stood by me during the times
when nobody wanted to.
You've shown me miraculous and beautiful
things I thought were impossible.
You've taught me things a lifetime of
experience could never teach.
You've given me the gifts of life, love,
wisdom, and happiness.
Now that You have done all this, I can return
Your favor by loving, forgiving,
Standing by, showing, teaching, and
giving to Your people,
As You did for me.
God, help me to have peace of mind and a
sense of moral confidence to know

In my heart what is right and wrong.
Give me strength to make wise decisions,
And the courage to stand by my
convictions—even in the face of
adversity or pressure from peers.
Help me to be happy with myself and
the path I have taken.
And love me when I stray from what is right,
So that Your love may always be my guide.
This I pray in the most Holy Name of
Your Son, Jesus Christ, Amen.

The Journey

My God, my God, why have you abandoned me?
Why so far from my call for help,
From my cries of anguish?
My God, I call by day, but you do not answer;
By night, but I have no relief.
Yet you are enthroned as the Holy One,
You are the glory of Israel.
In you our ancestors trusted,
They trusted and you rescued them.
To you they cried out and they escaped
and were not disappointed.
—Psalm 22:1–5
(United States Conference of Catholic Bishops)

At many crossroads in our life, God may seem to be far away. We may question where God is or has been in times of need, we may struggle to hear God's voice when we are seeking His direction in our lives, or we may feel distant from God if it has been a long time since we prayed. St. Augustine tells us that "our hearts are restless until they rest in You, oh Lord." We all experience a spiritual hunger and seek to find fullness in our lives through God in different ways.

The journey to God is unique for each person. Although it is sometimes overwhelming, especially if one has not traveled the path to God lately, it is a journey that we need not travel alone, and we can learn from the wisdom and experience of others who have traveled the same journey before. We each need to learn how and where we can approach our God on this journey through life, and to do so with trusting love. Matthew Kelly tells us that virtue is essential to the journey of the soul. "When we connect the good and noble external acts of our lives with positive internal attitudes and intentions, we grow in virtue" (Kelly 2002). Our journey can be somewhat discouraging if we do not feel particularly close to God, even for those who have spent a number of years trying. Some people measure their closeness to God in terms of whether or not they experience something extraordinary each time they pray or attend a religious service. If this is not the case, they may feel that their relationship with God is at a low point—and this may not be the case at all. We must learn to be patient. Even the lives of the saints tell us about the years of confusion, discouragement, and chaos that preceded their closeness to God. Some people also mistakenly feel that they cannot be close to God unless they have a total distaste and aversion for sin and can do no wrong. Holiness is not always black and white, and people striving toward holiness struggle with gray areas all the time with situations that can be a far cry from perfection. "Be patient, therefore, my brothers, until the coming of the Lord. See how the farmer awaits the precious yield of the soil. He looks forward to it patiently while the soil receives the winter and the spring rains" (James 5:7). Learn to be patient and trust in the Lord, especially while the soil is not yet yielding fruit.

It is absolutely essential that we begin our journey of service in the only place from which it is safe to proceed—in the Lord. While it is a good thing to be doing holy work, if we do holy work before we are in the Lord, we will have no heart for it and it will not be pleasing to our God. "For it is written, 'you shall worship the Lord your God, and Him only shall you serve'" (Matt. 4:10). Our God must be our refuge. We must totally rely upon Him and be obedient to Him and become His image to those we serve. We must live so that we do everything in the name of Jesus Christ. In our walk with God, we must never lose sight of our true goal—to allow our God to work in us and through us without our trying to interfere with His plan.

Service and suffering are often companions, and rarely do we see the full impact of our service. Our journey through life's many experiences is a journey filled with numerous opportunities. It is a journey based on giving and sharing our love; it is a journey of service to others. There can be no greater meaning to our journey than that of being a servant to others. We are here to take the path of service to others in order to fulfill that innate desire to make things better for those around us, to become one with others, to share our love and gifts with others. We must learn to serve and not have to be served. Matthew Kelly tells us that "every journey towards something is a journey away from something else if we turn back to God. At this moment in our lives, we also need to turn away from whatever leads us away from God" (Kelly 2002). On our journey, God has given our souls the capacity to see and to love and to feel other people's pain and needs. It is a journey based on giving and sharing your love; it is a journey of service to others. All souls share this innate desire to serve, and there are many paths that you will cross with souls that will allow you the opportunity to serve, even if only by a smile or an encouraging word or a pat on the back. The path of service to others should always be one of humility and compassion and mercy and sharing and love. It should never be one of boastfulness or bragging or pride. And so our Lord tells us, "Whoever serves Me must follow Me; and where I am, My servant also will be. My Father will honor the one who serves me" (John 12:26).

Mother Angelica tells us, "If you want to do something for the Lord, do it. Whatever you feel needs to be done, even if you are shaking in your boots and you're scared to death, take the first step. The grace comes with the first step. Being afraid is not the problem—it's doing nothing when you're afraid, that's the problem" (Arroyo 2007). The path of service will present itself in new and diverse ways that can never be predicted or foreseen. Each opportunity of service may present itself in a new and foreign way and will many times come unannounced and unexpected. It will simply be present to us, and we must decide in an instant whether we will take the opportunity presented to us and answer the call to serve, or whether we will hesitate and perhaps lose forever the moment and our opportunity to serve. Although there is an adolescent notion that freedom is the ability to do whatever you want, wherever you want, and whenever you want without interference from any authority, this is not true. Freedom instead is the strength of character to do what is good and what is right and what is noble. It is the good works of men—not their intentions, not their jobs, not their boasting, but their good works—which will be the evidence of the grace given to them. God will greatly reward the good works of men; and what a joy it will be to hear God say at the time of our death, "Well done, good and faithful servant" (Matt. 25:23).

So as to successfully walk the path of serving others, we must totally fulfill our quest of being who we were created to be and doing that for which we were created—with every thought and every word and every action. Service to others is the very purpose of our lives. It is that which sustains life and that which sustains love. In order to love, you must be free—free to give of yourself completely and without reservation. But to be able to give yourself freely to another person or to God or to a cause, you must first possess yourself and be free, and this freedom comes only through discipline. "I am the way, the truth and the life" (John 14:6)—for every person in every place. Along your journey, you must constantly become more like Jesus Christ. You must strive to live the Gospel and to become more like Jesus Christ. "As each soul journeys toward its individual destiny, God employs that soul to touch others, to serve others, and to inspire others to make their own journey" (Kelly 2002).

> *Dear good and gracious God!*
> *Awaken in us Your love and Your light.*
> *Make us aware of the journey*
> *   You will have us take,*
> *The reason for our existence,*
> *The way that we must take,*
> *And the path that we must follow to*
> *   make that journey to You.*
> *Let us see in every human being their*
> *   need for love and help.*
> *Let us look upon every human being*
> *   whose path we cross,*
> *And see a person equal to us in all things.*
> *And let us, in our humble and loving*
> *   way, see Your face in their face,*

And do unto them what we would do unto You.
We ask this all in the most holy name of
Jesus Christ, Your Son, Amen.

The Call of God

Then I heard the voice of the Lord saying,
"Whom shall I send? Who will go for us?"
"Here I am," I said; "Send me!"
—Isaiah 7:8

G od's call to us is not part of our own nature. Our affinities and choices and personal dispositions cannot be taken into account when God's call to us is not part of our own nature. As long as we think only about what we could best do to serve our God, we will never hear the call of God. We must first have a deep desire to do that which our God has in store for us to do. As Matthew Kelly says, "The unfathomable adventure begins when we stop asking, 'What's in it for me?' and turn humbly to God in our hearts and ask, 'How may I serve? What work do You wish me to do with my life? What is Your will for my life?'" (Kelly 2002). When we first die to self and allow ourselves to be brought into a personal relationship with Jesus Christ and become attuned to Him, and when we give up trying to listen to ourselves and second-guess what it is we are supposed to be doing, we will have an ear to hear what God tells us. "Let us therefore give ourselves to God with a great desire to begin to live thus, and beg Him to destroy in us the life of the world of sin, and to establish His life within us" (St. John Eudes, 1601–80). When we pray and adore and worship Jesus Christ, we cannot help but fall in love with Him; and His love, in turn, heals us and calms us and energizes us and strengthens us and gives us hope and confidence. It fills us with a peace inside of us that we are loved and that the arms of Jesus Christ will be around us and hold us close to His heart. To be brought into the zone of the call of our God is to be profoundly changed. God's call to us is not a call to any particular service. Putting ourselves in God's presence and dying to self may make us realize what we would like to do for Him. Service to others is the spillover of our extraordinary love and devotion to God. It should be a natural part of our lives. It is when God gets us into a relationship with Him that we understand His call and then do things for others out of utter and complete love for Him. To serve man and our God then becomes our intentional and conscious gift of love as a result of hearing God's call. When we hear and answer the call of God, we serve Him in the ordinary and menial ways of life out of pure and total devotion to Him. Service is not imposing our will on others—it is finding out what people need and then trying to help them do it.

I believe that we may lead lives worthy of the Lord, fully pleasing to Him, bearing fruit in every good work. And as we grow in the knowledge of God, through prayer and adoration, we become aware of not only God's love for us, but also of His sadness over those who reject Him or who have never heard of Him. This knowledge should move us to answer His call and say, "Here I am, Lord, I come to do Your will" (Isaiah 6:8). It makes us aware that we should not only be holy, but we should also be as a light to everyone we meet. We must open our eyes to the poor, to the oppressed, to those in despair, to the lonely, to the fearful, to the suffering, to the forgotten, to the homeless, to the imprisoned. The Holy Spirit orders us to love Jesus Christ so much that we feel absolutely compelled to be His servant so that when we come before Jesus Christ and ask for His mercy, He will remember the mercy we showed to His children in need and give us His mercy abundantly.

Josh Groban wrote a beautiful song entitled "What Is Our Service to Be?"

> *You raise me up so that I can stand on mountains,*
> *You raise me up so to walk on stormy seas.*
> *I am strong when I am on Your shoulders,*
> *You raise me up to more than I can be.*

> *Dear good and gracious God!*
> *Raise us up so we can stand on mountains,*
> *Make us strong to be Your servant.*
> *Raise us up to become Your hands,*
> *Make us an instrument of Your love.*
> *We ask this all in the most Holy Name of*
> *Jesus Christ, Your Son, Amen.*

Preparing to Serve

Who then is the faithful and prudent servant,
Whom the master has put in
charge of his household
To distribute to them their food at the proper time?
Blessed is that servant whom his master
on his arrival finds doing so.
But if that wicked servant says to himself,
'My master is delayed,' and begins
to beat his fellow servants
And eats and drinks with drunkards,
The master of that servant will come on a day when
He does not expect him and at an
hour he does not know,
And will cut him in pieces and put
him with the hypocrites.

In that place, there will be weeping
and gnashing of teeth."
—Matthew 24:45–51

The "master" represents Christ, the "blessed servant" represents faithful believers, and the "evil
servant" represents nonbelievers. Human life is portrayed as a stewardship in which the servants are
given oversight and responsibility for their master's
possessions. The master's goods represent time, tal-
ent, resources, and opportunities with which God
entrusts us. Since everything we have was given to
us by God, we are accountable for how we manage
what He gives us, and the time will come when each
of us will have to give our God an accounting. The
"blessed servant" is the one found doing what the
master had ordered. He is greatly rewarded by the
master. The "evil servant" is the nonbeliever who
does not believe in the master's return and, therefore,
has a false sense of security in his evil behavior. The
truth portrayed by the evil servant is that everyone
will have to give an accounting to God for the deeds
of this life—even people who refuse to acknowledge
the existence of God. He gave them life and all their

possessions and abilities. There is nothing that they have that was not given to them by their God. They too are His stewards. The "wailing and grinding of teeth" refers to the endless sorrow and torment of hell portrayed by those remorseful of squandered and wasted opportunities to serve others and their God.

There are those that say they are not worthy to be God's servants—that they are of no use where they are. But we certainly can be of no use where we are not! Always be willing to do what God asks you to do. To follow Jesus Christ does not only mean to do what He said; it means to do what He did—serve the poor, accept people as they are, show mercy, love everyone. We are all worthy in the eyes of our God. We were all created to serve—that is our very purpose in life. The call of God is not for just a special few—it is for everyone. Whether we hear God's call depends entirely upon how we listen, and what we hear depends upon our disposition and openness to listen and hear. All are called but only those who are willing to enter into a relationship with Jesus Christ, whose dispositions and attitudes have been changed and their ears opened, will hear the still, gentle voice of our God asking, "Who will go for me?" God does not single out a man or woman and say, "You go—I want you to serve me." We have to get over the common notion that God comes with pleading and force. If we but allow the Holy Spirit to bring us face-to-face with our God, we too will hear the gentle urging voice of God and in our perfect free will say, "Here I am, Lord, I come to do Your will." We are all called to serve and to do it with all our might. We must remember that our God does not call only people of means to do His will—He calls on us all and then gives us the means. Mother Angelica tells us that "God will often give to the very weak what the very strong have refused. When a strong man refuses to obey God, He turns to the weak" (Arroyo 2007). She goes on to say that "Simple and weak people are so conscious of their inadequacies that they depend upon God and they face the truth; a truth that proclaims, 'I can do all things in Him who strengthens me'" (Arroyo 2007).

Service does not have to be grand—even a smile, even very small acts of kindness—are looked upon as a service to others. For it is not how grand our service is to others that determines how great we are in the eyes of God, but with how much love we perform that service. Sometimes the greatest hindrance in our spiritual life is that we will look for the grand things to do. "Jesus took a towel and tied it around His waist. Then he poured water into a basin and began to wash the disciples' feet and dry them with the towel around His waist" (John 13:4–5). Toil and hard work are the criteria of true character. There are many times when our greatest service has no grandeur, no illumination, no hoopla, no thrill. It is just a grind, a common task, totally boring. We must learn to live in the domain of drudgery. If we obey our calling from God to serve as He would have us serve, then the tiniest detail in which we serve and obey has all the omnipotent power of the grace of God behind it! Remember that "the Lord measures our perfection in anything not by the multitude nor the magnitude of our deeds, but by the manner in which we perform them" (St. John of the Cross, 1542–91).

How does one prepare to go out into the world and make a difference, to go into the world and serve others, to go out into the world and make a positive impact on those whose lives we cross? We must realize that our life begins and ends at the altar of God in prayer. Though we do not all have grand talents and abilities we can offer to others, we have those gifts that our God has given us, the gifts our God wants us to have. It is what we do with what is given to us that is important—not how grand our gifts are. "God bestows more consideration on the purity of intention with which our actions are performed than on the actions themselves" (St. Augustine, 354–430). We must all be "blessed servants in the eyes of our God, and use the gifts and resources and talents our master has given us to do good for others. We must remember that an action of small value performed with much love of God is far more excellent than one of a higher virtue, done with less love of God" (St. Francis de Sales, 1567–1622). Jesus took a towel and washed the feet of His disciples. If one is so blessed by the Lord, he or she has to act as God would— with love, mercy, and justice (Amos 6:7–15). Once blessed by God, we are obligated to treat others as God has treated us. God loves everyone and we, in turn, are expected to do the same. "Remember that anything is small in the eyes of God. Do all that you can do with love" (St. Therese of Lisieux, 1873–97). We show our love for Him by loving one another, and God is in every one of us. Jesus was very definite on this point: "This I command you, to love one another" (John 15:17). Isaiah, the prophet, tells us: "Behold, my servant shall prosper, he shall be exalted and lifted up, and shall be very high" (Isaiah 53).

Each and every day, we have the opportunity to touch the lives of others, to bring joy to someone, to ease someone's pain, to share our light with another human being. This is the true meaning of service, the true meaning of compassion. Do not let a day slip away without taking advantage of your opportunities to serve and to bring dignity into the life of someone else (Arroyo 2007). Make your motto, "As for me and my house, we will serve the Lord" (Josh. 24:15).

Dear good and gracious God
We come before You in humility and love.
Let us die to self and open our hearts to
what You would have us do.
Give us the knowledge of Your will for us,
The courage to follow Your will,
And the grace to fulfill it.
We ask this all in the most Holy Name of
Jesus Christ, Your Son, Amen.

On First Becoming a Saint

May the God of peace Himself make you perfectly holy,
And may you entirely, spirit, soul, and body,
Be preserved blameless for the coming
of our Lord Jesus Christ,
The one who calls you is faithful,
And He will also accomplish it.
—1 Thessalonians 5:23 (Roman Catholic Bible)

Mother Angelica tells us that "a saint is one who empties himself and takes on the image of Jesus, so that the person and Jesus are look-alikes" (Arroyo 2007). It is no more than being "a frail human being keeping the commandments" (Arroyo

2007). To become a saint, you must suffer much. Matthew Kelly describes a saint as "a person who is the holiest person he can be, and to be holy is to become fully the person God created you to be." He goes onto say that "personal holiness is the answer to every problem" (Kelly 2002). The ultimate sign of a Christian is that we are willing to abandon our own wills and become an absolute slave of Jesus Christ. Until we do that, we cannot begin to become a saint. Our service to others must be done when God commands it—not in our time, but in God's time. It is amazing how much we debate and argue and find excuses for not doing it right away. A true saint never considers not following God's command to serve. True saints abandon feeling sorry for themselves and never allow the feeling of being used or taken advantage of in their service to the poor to enter in. The true test of living the life of a saint is not recognition or success or glory—it is faithfulness in life as it really is. True saints allow God to use them as His hands and feet. Being a saint means passionate and total concentration on God's holy will and His point of view. It means every power of our body, soul, and spirit imprisoned and kept for God's purpose only. It is the goal of getting as close to God as you can. It means being made one with Jesus Christ so that the disposition that ruled Him will rule us as well. It is someone who will ask God to make them as holy as He can make a sinner saved by His grace. The life of a saint is filled with struggles and is always a process—sometimes a lifelong process. What separates a saint from an ordinary person is the saint's constant struggle for holiness. Every man and every woman is called to holiness, regardless of life's circumstances. "Holiness is the goal of the Christian life and our essential purpose" (Kelly 2002). As Oscar Wilde so eloquently put it, "every saint has a past and every sinner has a future."

Why are you not a saint? It is either that you do not want to be a saint or that you do not believe God can make you one. Holiness is for everyone and is compatible with every state of life. One of the greatest hindrances in coming to Jesus Christ is the excuse of our temperament. We make our temperament and our natural affinities barriers to coming to Christ. But the first thing we realize when we do come to Christ is that He pays no attention whatsoever to our natural affinities. It is a matter of completely emptying ourselves and allowing Jesus Christ to work through us.

The true mark of a saint is the moral originality, which comes from the awesome spirit of God springing up in us. "Our business is to love what God would have done. He wills our vocation as it is. Let us love that and not trifle away our time hankering after other people's vocations" (St. Francis de Sales, 1567–1622). The saint is the person who realizes that it is God who gives us everything we need to serve Him. It is those people that come to this realization and give themselves totally into God's hands that our Lord will call and who will be able to go out into the world echoing to others the call of Christ. The absolute imprint of a saint is that he or she is willing to waive their own rights and totally obey the Lord Jesus. The saint is someone in whom pride and selfishness have been completely erased. Once again, I quote Matthew Kelly in what he says about a saint: "The goal of the Christian life is holiness. Those who have attained this goal we call saints. They have found their essential purpose, they have pursued their essential purpose, they have celebrated their essential purpose. The saints followed the great Spiritual North Star, they have quietly chiseled away at the defects and weaknesses in their characters, they have become the best version of themselves. They have truly applied themselves to the Christian life. They have brought the Gospel to life, and they have lived authentic lives" (Kelly 2002).

Our Lord exhorts us to be generous in helping all human beings. "The surest signs of holiness are an insatiable desire to improve oneself and an unquenchable concern for unholy people. Holiness is to allow each moment to be all it can be" (Kelly 2002). We cannot walk or not walk according to our natural likes and dislikes. We all have some people that we like and some people that we do not like. But we must never allow those likes and dislikes to rule in our Christian life. We must pay attention to the people that God brings around us, and we will be humiliated to find that this is His way of telling us the kind of person we have been to Him. Striving for holiness means to continually grasp the circumstances we call *moments* and use then to change and grow, and allow God to transform us into all He has created us to be. The things that Jesus did were most tedious and menial—it is these very things that we do that can be most important in the eyes of our God if performed out of total love for the Lord and his people. "If I then, your Lord and Master, has washed your feet, ye also ought to wash one another's feet" (John 13:14).

Continually tell yourself that the purpose of your life is not wealth or happiness or good health, but holiness.

God has created me to do him
some definite service. He has
committed some work to me
which He has not committed
to another. I have my mission.
I may never know it in this life,
but I shall be told it in the next.
I am a link in a chain, a bond of
connection between persons. He
has not created me for naught.
I shall do good—I shall do His
work. I shall be an angel of peace,
a preacher of truth in my own
place while not intending it, if I
do but keep His commandments.
Therefore, I will trust Him,
whatever I am, I can never be
thrown away. If I am in sickness,
my sickness may serve Him. In
perplexity, my perplexity may
serve Him. If I am in sorrow, my
sorrow may serve Him. He does
nothing in vain. He knows what
He is about. He may take away
my friends. He may throw me
among strangers. He may make

> me feel desolate, make my spirits
> sink, hide my future from me—
> still, HE KNOWS WHAT HE IS
> ABOUT. (John Henry Newman;
> emphasis added)

In order to serve others and to do it with joy, we must first strive in all things to become a saint. "There is nothing quite so important in the daily life of a Christian as the need to shine before men with the light of good example" (author unknown). Holiness is "simply the application of the values and principles of the Gospel to the circumstances of our everyday lives—one moment at a time" (Kelly 2002). It is said that the only difference between an ordinary person and a saint is that a saint is an ordinary person who keeps getting up after falling down in the eyes of God and strives always to do better. One cannot become holy and thus become a saint until we truly open our hearts and strive always to see the absolute awesome and unfathomable beauty of God in everything around us. There is a beautiful Jewish tradition to each day thank God for at least ten gifts. "Thank you, God, for letting me wake up." "Thank you, God, for the rain." "Thank you, God, for the sun and its warmth." "Thank you, God, for the breath of life today." "Thank you, God, for the flowers." "Thank you, God for my children." "Thank you, God, for my job." "Thank you, God, for my friends." "Thank you, God for being able to talk," etc. Start this tradition in your life and daily become more and more aware of just how great and awesome our God is. Though God does not really need our gratitude, we need to be grateful. "Gratitude itself is a wholesome and healing force," says a mediation from the book One Day at a Time in Al-Anon (Al-Anon Family Group 1988). A thankful heart not only deepens our faith, but also enhances the quality of our lives. We need to turn to God on sunny good days, as well as when we are in the depths of despair. How can we be grateful regardless of life's circumstances? We must count our simple blessings. Focus on your simple gifts and conveniences—friends, family, food, health, running water, electricity, pets, even special talents and education. The list is endless. As you count your blessings, give thanks.

Every day, review your simple praise list. Take time to thank God for faithfulness, for all your material gifts, for God's refusal to give up on you. And when prayers are answered, recognize this as well. Focus on the positive things in your life and the lives of those around you. By focusing on the positive things, sometimes the bad do not seem so unbearable. Start looking down the ladder instead of up. That way, things get put in perspective as you see how much better off you are than many others and how much higher on the social and financial ladder you are. Try to start a healthy habit of optimistic thinking. Focus on just one blessing each day. You could begin by posting a sign on your refrigerator or mirror. "Today, I am grateful for…" Every day, fill in the blank with one positive aspect in your life or have family members take turns filling in the blank. "I am grateful for the phone call from my daughter," wrote the mother who had a fight with her daughter two weeks ago. "I am grateful for having my baby in her car seat today," wrote the mother who was in a fender bender that day. "I am grateful for finding my puppy," wrote the ten-year-old girl. The list goes on and on. Or suggest to your family before dinner that each person at the table thank God for one good thing in their life that day. We should try always "to embrace life with both arms wide open, to lay our lives enthusiastically at the service of humanity, to love deeply the people who cross our paths, and above all, to embrace our God. Life should never be wasted, not one moment, because life is precious" (Kelly 2002). The simple secret of a saint's life is that "a saint's love does not ask about deservingness, or rewards, or consequences. It does not ask anything. It just loves" (Kreeft, 1990).

Dear good and gracious God!
Help us to always see You as our loving Father.
Help us to empty ourselves completely and
 liberate us from all that keeps us from You.
Help us to do the will of the Father,
In our relationships with others, in our
 homes, at our work, in the streets,
And wherever we may meet our
 fellow human beings.
Let us be recognized not by our
 boasting or bragging,
But in the gentleness that we display,
So that they may know that we
 work with the Lord.
Come into our hearts and heal us.
 Help us to forgive ourselves and others.
We ask this all in the most holy name of
 Jesus Christ, Your Son, Amen.

The Call to Holiness

Sanctify yourselves, then, and be holy;
For I, the Lord, your God, am holy.
I, who have set you apart from the
other nations to be My own.
—Leviticus 20:7–8

"Whatever you do, work at it with all your heart, as working for the Lord, not for men, since you know that you will receive an inheritance from the Lord as a reward. It is the Lord Christ you are serving" (Colos. 3:23–24). "Turn yourself round like a piece of clay and say to the Lord, 'I am clay, and You, Lord, the potter. Make of me what You will'" (Blessed John of Avila, 1500–1569). Mother Angelica says that "holiness consists of four words— the will of God" (Arroyo 2002).

God's destiny for all of mankind is holiness and to experience His salvation. We are called to be holy, no matter what our vocation in life is. If we are nurses, we are called to be *holy* nurses; if we are teachers, we are called to be *holy* teachers; if we are attorneys, we are called to be *holy* attorneys; if we are politicians, we are called to be *holy* politicians; if we are mothers, we are called to be *holy* mothers; if we are mechanics, we are called to be *holy* mechanics. Whatever our calling in life, it is meant to be a *holy* calling. We must constantly remind ourselves and others that holiness is within our reach. Matthew Kelly tells us that "holiness is simply the application of the values and principles of the Gospel under the circumstances of our every-day lives—one moment at a time…. The surest signs of holiness are an insatiable desire to improve oneself and an unquenchable concern for unholy people" (Kelly 2007). If you have done poorly up until now, start today to love and serve the Lord. Let yourself become a person of mercy. First repent of your sins and ask for God's mercy. Then start today to strive to love and serve the Lord and your neighbor. Your conscience is a gift of God's mercy calling a person to repent and convert. It is an instrument of God's mercy to become converted and ask for God's forgiveness. To whom much is given, much will be expected. "Oh good and faithful servant, welcome into My kingdom," says the Lord. Ask God to teach us to obey Him willingly and promptly and to teach us to serve with a good and upright heart. Remember that holiness is simply the balance between what we want and the law of our God. We must learn to push away the things that come against us and go against the law of God and, in that way, we will not fear opposition to God's will. "None of us is perfect….Every day, we can make a choice to be like Jesus instead of like ourselves. Every day, we have a chance to transform our soul. Keep trying. Holiness and virtue are a slow process" (Arroyo 2002).

God's aim is for all of His creatures to become saints. But no one can enter into the realm of being a saint without first burying their old lives and resurrecting in the life of Jesus Christ. There is no working for salvation. It is only by Jesus Christ dying on the cross and paying the price for our sins that we are saved, that we have salvation, that God allows us to become holy. "But sanctification means more than deliverance from sin, it means the deliberate commitment of myself whom God has saved to God, and that I do not care what it costs" (Chambers 1963). The rule of thumb to follow in our desire to become holy is to do nothing that you would not do if you thought God was watching you. Everything you do should be done in the light of the final judgment of God, knowing that at the end of the world, all will know even your most secret sins and thoughts and deeds.

But after we have accepted God as our Lord and Savior and received His salvation, then He expects us to serve Him. Every single believer has at least one gift that can be used in God's service. You must give where God delivers you to give and where it will be honoring to Him. We should never make excuses or tolerate for any reason, either in ourselves or in others, any practice that is not in keeping with a holy God. Holiness means unblemished walking with our feet, unblemished working with our hands, unblemished talking with our mouths, unblemished seeing with our eyes, and unblemished thinking with our minds. Every part of our lives must be under the constant scrutiny and watchfulness of our God and should be able to pass the test of His will. A Christian servant of God must be ready to face Jesus at every turn, and we must remember that Jesus does not come where or when we expect Him. Instead, He appears where we least expect Him and always in the least likely of circumstances. God's servant must expect Jesus at every turn and always be ready. Holiness should manifest to others what our God has given us. Our Lord told us, "For I say to you, that unless your righteousness shall exceed the righteousness of the Scribes and Pharisees, you shall not by any means enter the kingdom of heaven" (Matt. 5:20). In other words, we must be holier than the most holy person we know, we must be more moral than the most moral person we know, and we must be more ethical than the most ethical person we know. We must beware of allowing our differences to hinder our walk in love with one another. And we must beware of not acting upon what we see and hear in our moments with our God on the mount. "Walk while you have the light, so that darkness does not overcome you" (John 12:35). If we fail to obey the light, it will surely turn into darkness. If we waiver even slightly regarding the things our God has revealed to us in light about our sanctification in life, it is like becoming rotten in our spiritual lives. When we become a saint, we call all men and women friends, and we enter into friendships based on the new life created in us, which has absolutely no affinity with our old life, but only with the life of our God. It is a life that is totally pure and humble and devoted to the work and love of God. It is "when we pursue what is good, true, beautiful and noble, with honesty and integrity, that we become holy" (Kelly 2002).

New life in Christ manifests itself in conscious repentance and sorrow for our sins and unconscious holiness. Our attitude as a saint should not be to ask our God for deliverance from all difficulties and sorrow, but that we be preserved in the fires of difficulties and recognize that all gold is tested by fire. A sanctified soul is a soul that is of profound humble holiness, a holiness based on painful repentance and sorrow for sin, and a sense of unspeakable shame and guilt; and one that realizes amazingly that God's total love for us, despite our lack of love for Him, has completed everything for our salvation and sanctification. Sanctification makes us one with our God— how totally awesome is that!

Becoming a saint means not our idea of what we want our God to do for us—it is instead God's idea of what He wants to do for us. It means that the holiness of Jesus Christ is manifest in us. It is Christ in us. It is the qualities of our God in us—His holiness, His love, His patience, His humility, His purity, His faith, His compassion, His mercy for all. We must become of the mind-set mentally and spiritually that we will allow Him to sanctify us wholly at any cost. We must open the eyes of our hearts to hear the gentle voice of the Holy Spirit as He whispers His guidance and directions to us. In order to hear the quiet voice of the Spirit, we must live in perfect communion with our God. As Matthew Kelly says, "Holiness brings us to life. Holiness refines every human ability. Holiness doesn't dampen our emotions, it elevates our emotions. Those who possess holiness are the most joy-filled people in history.... Holiness is to allow each moment to be all it can be....Strive to become and remain spiritually tenacious! Just so, the Son of Man did not come to be served but to serve and to give His life as a ransom for many" (Kelly 2002). Let us come to realize that Jesus Christ has served us in all of our needs—in our sinfulness, in our selfishness, in our meanness, in our disobedience—and let us become like Christ to others. In the book of Micah 6:8, it says: "You have been told what is good and what Yahweh wants of us. Only this, that you live justly, love tenderly, and walk humbly with your God."

God gives us an intrinsic knowledge to know justice from injustice. He puts this knowledge in our hearts and makes our hearts yearn for what is right, even though we sometimes do little more than ignore the whisperings in our heart that speak against injustice. Our challenge is to suppress our pride and fear, to listen to the whisperings in our heart, and to act on injustice following the will of God.

So, too, just as we intrinsically know what is just and what is not, we also know how to love tenderly. We are always given the choice to choose love or pride, to choose love or jealously, to choose love or revenge, to choose love or selfishness. We know how to love tenderly, but we must *choose* to do so. To make justice win over injustice and to love tenderly, we must first walk humbly with our God, allowing God to take us by the hand and lead us to doing that which is just, that which He has in store for us to do, and that which will allow us to love tenderly. This alone will cause us to be deeply and surely fulfilled and happy. Matthew Kelly tells us: "This is what is required to walk humbly with God. The candle is within you. When you have learned to carry and protect it, then you will be able to live justly—choose what is good, just, true, and noble in every situation—and love tenderly" (Kelly 2002). And remember that holiness is a lifelong process that does not end once we attain it. Holiness is within our reach. It is not something unattainable. It can be as simple as knowing when to say yes and when to say no. We must fix our sights on

God and God alone and realize that doing the will of God will bring us to that state in life called holiness. "In the world, whenever you give something away, you lose it. But in the spiritual life, in the life of holiness, whatever you give comes back to you again and again, and it grows and multiples. Think of a star in the sky. I see it and point it out to you. When you look at it, I have not lost it. I still have the star, and the joy of it, and something more: I have the joy of you beside me" (Arroyo 2007).

Dear good and gracious God!
Let us today commit to You to become the
        holiest person we can become.
Let us recognize that it is You
        manifest in us that is holy,
And that without You we cannot find sanctity.
Let us strive to achieve perfection through
        our consecration to You,
And be always willing to go where
        You send us and say,
"Here I am, Lord, I come to do Your will."
We ask this all in the most holy name of
        Jesus Christ, Your Son, Amen.

Discipline

If your brother sins against you,
Go and show him his fault, just
between the two of you.
If he listens to you, you have won your brother over.
But if he will not listen,
Take one or two others along,
So that every matter may be established by
the testimony of two or three witnesses.
If he refuses to listen to them,
Tell it to the church.
And if he refuses to listen even to the church,
Treat him as you would a pagan or a tax collector.
—Matthew 18:15–17

Self-discipline is necessary for anyone to serve God and his fellow man. It is something that is not comfortable for many and something that many fear. Peter Finley Dunne once pointed out that Jesus Christ "came to comfort the afflicted but also to afflict the comfortable." Self-discipline calls on us and challenges us to take on the spirit of God through self-discipline and, in so doing, discard or reject the spirit of the world as we know it. Self-discipline is feared and unpopular because it is looked upon as something that is used to tyrannize a person or make a person do something they do not want to do. It is actually quite the contrary. As Matthew Kelly puts it, "Discipline is the faithful friend who will introduce you to your true self. Discipline is the worthy protector who will defend you from your lesser self. And discipline is the extraordinary mentor who will challenge you to become the best version of yourself and all God created you to do" (Kelly 2002). Self-discipline is a thing of beauty. It is something we must possess before we possess genius. Everyone we know who has become great is a master of self-discipline—Ali, Picasso, Mozart, Tiger Woods, Mother Teresa, ad infinitum. First, self-discipline—then genius…With discipline, we are confined to soulless living and must content ourselves with work, food, momentary worldly pleasures, and anything that can help distract us from the misery of purposeless living. Without discipline, the soul dies. Slowly perhaps, but surely" (Kelly 2002).

Each of us has been placed on this earth for some specific purpose, "but without discipline, you will never discover that purpose. Without discipline, you will march slowly and surely to join Thoreau's masses living a life of quiet desperation" (Kelly 2002).

To allow us to share in His happiness, Christ invites us to a life of discipline. The way to the fullness of life that Jesus Christ invites us to is through discipline. Matthew Kelly tells us that "there are four major aspects of the human person—physical, emotional, intellectual, and spiritual…" (Kelly 2002). As each soul makes the journey, God uses that soul to touch others, to serve others, to heal others, to inspire others to make their own journey toward Him. He uses each soul to make a difference in the hearts and minds and lives of those He puts on our path. He uses each of us to help light the path of those people He sends to us in our lives. We must be self-disciplined in our own physical, emotional, intellectual, and spiritual aspects of our lives in order to help others in those aspects of their lives. When we devote some time each day to enhancing the four aspects of the human person, then we will become strengthened in those areas of our lives, and we will be able to share those strengths with those less fortunate, the poor, the underprivileged, the anxious, the fearful, the abandoned, the rejected, the depressed, the lonely, the poor of spirit. Discipline yourselves in all areas of your life, and you will receive the fullness of Christ that He promised. Discipline yourselves in the things of our God, and you will become strengthened like never before, to go out into the world and make a difference. Open your heart to God's will for you, and you will become a true servant of the Lord.

Dear good and gracious God!
We ask for Your help in becoming
        motivated and strong,
In becoming a follower of Christ as we
        pursue our true purpose in life.
We ask that You speak loudly to us so that
        we hear Your gentle encouragement.
We ask that You allow us to hear Your whisper,
And we ask that You give us the courage to
        act on Your encouraging words.
So that we may master the art of self-discipline
And, in so doing, will attain our purpose in life.
And we ask this all in the most holy name
        of Jesus Christ, Your son, Amen.

Obedience to Our God

Do you not know that when you present
yourselves to someone as obedient slaves,
You are slaves of the one you obey,
Either of sin, which leads to death, or of
obedience, which leads to righteousness?
—Romans 6:16–23

Most of us do not consciously disobey our God—we simply choose to ignore His commandments. We sometimes put a question mark where God puts a period. We want to serve our God, but only in an advisory position. It is not that our path is not clearly laid out for us through God's word—it is simply that we choose not to heed what He tells us to do and not to do. We make excuses, we justify our actions by saying that everybody else is doing it, we do not think something is bad if it does not hurt someone else. For some, we believe that we are walking in the light of Christ if we walk as other people walk. We set our standards according to the standards of those we respect or like or idolize. We do not realize that if we give the devil a ride, he will always want to drive. The deadliest fantasy today is not hypocrisy but unconscious denial. The penalty of sin is that one gets used to it if we do it enough, and then our shame and guilt over it disappear. Our God tells us, "Slaves, obey your earthly masters with respect and fear, and with sincerity of heart, just as you would obey Christ, doing the will of God from your heart. Serve wholeheartedly, as if you were serving the Lord, not men, because you know that the Lord will reward everyone for whatever good he does, whether he is slave or free" (Eph. 6:5–9).

Obeying our God does not mean that we cannot sin—it means merely that if we obey the commands of the God within us, we need not sin. There is a constant inner struggle in us—our will against God's will. We simply will not be able to be a true servant of our God until we put to death our own wills. But we cannot reckon ourselves dead to sin until we reconcile the issue of dying to our will and living to God's. Choose to walk in the company of the holiest people you know for we become like those that surround us. And beware of triumphing with someone doing the wrong thing. Our God is quite clear in what He tells us: "If you love me, you will keep My commandments" (John 14:15). Once we open the eyes of our hearts and truly listen to our God, we realize that by ignoring His commandments, we have been disrespecting God, and we are filled with guilt and shame and humiliation because we have chosen not to heed Him. No one ever receives a word from God without constantly being put to the test over it. We hear God's gentle urging, we know His will, and we choose to disobey Him anyway. Disobedience and ignoring the word of God cause a spiritual death within us, so we should not wonder why we do not go on spiritually. "If you come to the altar and there you remember that you have sinned against your brother, leave your gift there in front of the altar. First go and be reconciled to your brother; then come and offer your gift" (Matt. 5:23–24). Sometimes God puts us into a sort of darkness where things do not go our way, or we are disappointed or afraid. He does this sometimes to teach us to listen to Him and obey. It is in the dark times of our lives that we must listen and not talk, listen and not act, listen and decide to make some changes, listen and be humble, listen and be sorry for ignoring our God, listen and become soft of heart to choose to do His will. "What I say to you in the darkness, speak in the light; what you hear whispered, proclaim on the housetops. And do not be afraid of those who kill the body but cannot kill the soul; rather, be afraid of the one who can destroy both soul and body in hell" (Matt. 10:27–28).

When we get a message through scripture, we should not ignore it. We must watch the things we choose to ignore and over which we shrug our shoulders, and then we will know why we do not go on spiritually. We must stop choosing to change God's message to our liking, and let God's message instead change us. We must obey all that God commands us to obey. We cannot live under the excuse of ignorance or innocence when it comes to obedience to our God. His teachings are clear and we must heed them if we expect to grow spiritually and not face the wrath of our God. He is a fair and just God, but we must recognize Him as the supreme authority. Jesus tells us that if we are to be His disciples, we must not only live right, but we must have righteous motives in all that we do—so pure and good that there will be nothing that needs to be censured. The Sermon on the Mount is not a set of rules and regulations, it is not a set of suggestions—it instead describes the lives we will lead when we live in obedience to our God and the Holy Spirit is alive in our hearts. We should never seek righteousness in the other man, but should instead never cease to look for justice in ourselves. Never search for justice, but never cease to live it. The command of our God is simple—"DO YOU LOVE ME? THEN FEED MY SHEEP. IF YOU WOULD BE MY DISCIPLE, YOU MUST BE DEVOTED TO ME " (John 21:15–17).

We must beware of those things that we brush off and say do not matter. In the eyes of our God, everything matters, and we will be held accountable for our actions, whether we justify them away or not. Some people feel like it is okay to take a holiday from morality or a holiday from spirituality. It is no more okay to take a holiday form morality or spirituality than it is okay to stop eating. It is like not feeding your body. If you stop feeding your body for a few weeks, your body dies; if you stop feeding your soul, your soul dies. Both need nourishment to stay healthy and alive. Do not forget this! Remember that God not only expects us to do His will, but He is in us to help us do it.

Dear good and gracious God!
Help us in our daily struggle to obey You.
In our times of weakness when
*   we stumble and fall,*
In our times when we feel scared and anxious,
In our times of hesitancy and resistance.
Give us the strength we need to do Your will,
The courage we need to get up when we fall,
The wisdom we need to know what is right,
And the peace to calm our fears.
We ask this all in the most Holy Name of
*   Jesus Christ, Your Son, Amen.*

Prayer

Have no anxiety at all, but in everything,
by prayer and petition,
And with thanksgiving, make your
requests known to God.
Then the peace of God that surpasses all understanding
Will guard your hearts and minds in Christ Jesus.
—Philippians 4:4–7

"Prayer is to take your failings, your evil tendencies and struggle with them" (Kelly 2002). Matthew Kelly tells us that: "In the final analysis, the measure of your life will be the measure of your prayer. Action without prayer is useless. Action that springs forth from prayer is the work of God" (Kelly 2002). Throughout the entire gospels, the disciples make only one request of Jesus—*"Lord, teach us to pray"* (John 11:1). We must continuously ask God to teach us to pray as we yearn to be nearer to our God, to be in communion with Him, to know Him. Prayer is the highest expression of the Christian spirit of love and it is also its chief nourishment. "It is to our soul what rain is to the soil. Fertilize the soil ever so richly for it will remain barren unless fed by frequent rains" (St. John Vianney, 1786–1859). Prayer is a conversation with God who loves us and loves to talk to us and loves to embrace us with His all-encouraging love and mercy. St. Paul ardently prayed that we should all go to the Lord and seek His wisdom and revelation so that we might become holy, bear fruit for Him, and be strengthened by Him. He said that it does not matter if you are the holiest Christian or the weakest and most disordered of believers. Everyone who comes to Jesus Christ will be rewarded and blessed (Col. 1:9–11).

St. Paul implores and instructs us to pray always and to pray unceasingly. Since we are children of God, we have immediate access to the Father and will be refused nothing. He tells us to pray without growing weary. Pray with great confidence and trust that we will be heard. "God is a spring of living water which flows unceasingly into the hearts of those who pray" (St. Louis de Montfort, 1673–1716). We must pray nonstop, and we must never be discouraged when we pray. We must pray in patience and we must pray in love. And we must always know in our hearts that our prayers will be answered in God's way and in God's time and in God's style, and we must trust that we will someday see the wisdom of God in how He answers our prayers. "The prayer of a humble soul penetrates the heavens and presents itself before the throne of God and does not leave without God's looking on it and hearing it. The prayer of him that humbleth himself shall pierce the clouds,…and he will not depart till the Most High behold" (Eccles. 35:21). Since we are baptized and receive the sacraments, our prayers are like incense to the Father— called by Christ as our intercessor. Through baptism, we are a new people of God, the new creation.

It is through the power of prayer that our hearts are opened and our barriers to love are broken down. It is through prayer that we are showered with God's unending love so that we will feel worthy to receive the gifts of the Holy Spirit. Everything we do in the name of Jesus Christ—working, playing, suffering, rejoicing, struggling, fearing—is meant to be an unceasing prayer. "When you start to think of prayer as Someone, you are finally able to speak to God" (Arroyo 2007). For we have become new people and our language is prayer. God loves us—we must be totally confident of that and of the power of prayer. Thus, we must pray unceasingly and in the total confidence that our prayers will be heard and answered because of God's unceasing love for us. And the good news is that God not only loves us but He loves all that for which we pray. Remember that he who kneels before God can stand before anyone. The other great news is that it is our very brokenness and sinfulness, which are the things that make us even more irresistible to our loving and merciful and compassionate God. Prayer will change our hearts in God's mind. The true miracle of prayer is not that God listens to us, but that our hearts are changed through God's love for us. "Prayer prepares us to get rid of all those things inside yourself that are not like Jesus" (Arroyo 2007).

We must pray for wisdom and for the other gifts of the Holy Spirit. It is in the wisdom of the Holy Spirit that we learn that true prayer comes from a loving relationship with a loving God. Through prayer comes confidence and perseverance—not from a sense of merit, but from a sense of humble trust. In this wisdom, we learn that true prayer is a gift. We learn that it is the spirit of Christ who really prays in us, and that we just need to surrender to the moment and in silence to recognize the agony of Jesus Christ in this wisdom. We also learn that true prayer is the acceptance of the truth—that we are loved by Christ unconditionally.

In this wisdom, we allow Christ's love to heal us and send us out in the urgency of love to tell others the good news. The good news is that God loves us and died for us and will never leave us. We must look at prayer as a necessity and not as an option, so that we can truly experience God's love in everything we think and do and say. Prayer is the highest expression of the Christian spirit of love, and it is its chief nourishment. Once again, pray unceasingly in the spirit of love.

God should become the center of our existence, so there should be no human activity, which cannot be offered to God to be made holy, pleasing, and acceptable to Him. St. Paul goes on to say, "With all prayer and supplication, pray at every opportunity in the Spirit.... For the Spirit too comes to the aid of our weakness; for we do not know how to pray as we ought, but the Spirit itself intercedes with inexpressible groanings for us. And the one who searches hearts knows what is the intention of the Spirit, because it intercedes for the holy ones according to God's will" (Rom. 8:26–27).

What is prayer? Prayer is the noblest expression of man, the very breath of the soul. It is as necessary as life itself. For many, prayer is quite formal and very repetitive, directed toward a God who is far away and far above us; a God who may or may not hear us; a God who may or may not answer us; a God who, to many, is someone we go to only in time of great need or sickness or fear or want; a God to be feared; a God who is impersonal and to be approached only with utmost formality and reverence.

Prayer is communicating with God—pure and simple. "O Lord, I call to you; come quickly to me. Hear my voice when I call to you. May my prayer be set before you like incense; may the lifting up of my hands be like the evening sacrifice" (Psalm 141:1–2). Prayer does not have to be formal, it does not have to be complicated, it does not have to be scary, and it does not have to be reserved only for times of need or fear or want or sickness. It is communicating with our loving and merciful and forgiving God, and asking for His help in all that we do. "Everything you do is for God, though your attention, your activity, is focused on the duties of life. This way, there is no separation between your life and your prayer; they are woven together like threads in a tapestry" (Arroyo 2007). Every honest act of kindness or act of work can be transformed into prayer by offering the actions of your life to God as a prayer. We must put our total trust in the Lord and pray with utmost confidence. We must pray unceasingly and know that our God hears us. He knows our innermost thoughts and fears and needs. He is there unconditionally, and He is there always. He does not judge, He does not ignore, He does not play favorites. In fact, He is drawn to sinners—those who come to Him with repentance and trust, those who ask His forgiveness, those who seek to do His will, those who were lost and seek Him again, those who die to self and realize that their God is waiting for them with open arms. "God will not hear our prayers unless we acknowledge ourselves to be sinners. We do this when we ponder on our own sins alone, and not on those of our neighbors" (St. Moses the Ethiopian, fourth century). Like the prodigal son was welcomed into his father's loving arms, so are God's children who were lost received into the loving arms of the Father. Our God does not ask questions, He does not place blame, He does not make us feel guilty, He does not care why we have sinned. He simply opens His arms and takes us back with total and unconditional love—how totally awesome is that! Our God is the one who loved us so much that He gave us His only Son to atone for our sins—there truly can be no greater love than that!

Our God is a holy and merciful and forgiving God. He knows our weaknesses and our brokenness; He knows our failings and our misgivings. He is a compassionate God. He loves us above all else despite our misgivings. There is nothing we can do or say that is not already forgiven, if we but repent of our sins and ask for God's forgiveness and mercy. What a beautiful and comforting feeling; what an unburdening of our heavy loads!

Most of us have grown up in the belief that the more we pray, the better off we will be; and the more we repeat certain prayers, the better. It is quite frightening to learn that what prayers we have mastered and practiced do not really matter; that those who have never turned to God are just as loved by God as we are; that no act of our own can insure God's favor; that God will never force us to make the right choices; that the only gift we can offer God is our broken, sinful selves; that God will sometimes bring into our lives strangers and expect us to treat them as our brothers and sisters; that God always offers us the very risky gift of freedom to make our own choices; and that we are totally powerless and needy in the eyes of God. But we must be hopeful and continue to pray, for it is in these fears that we receive the beginning of wisdom so that we can learn that true prayer comes from a relationship with a loving God and Father. "He who does not give up prayer cannot possibly continue to offend God habitually. Either he will give up prayer, or he will stop sinning" (St. Alphonsus Liguori, 1696–1787).

We must learn that true and powerful prayer can be spontaneous or formal, but that it must always come from the heart. We learn that true prayer comes from a relationship with a loving God and Father. We learn that true prayer is one that we pray in total confidence and with perseverance, not from a sense of our own merit, but from a sense of total humble trust in the Father. We are given the wisdom to learn that prayer can be personal (solitary and silent) or done in a community (very expressive and formal). And, yet, it will be the same Sprit *groaning within us*, teaching us what to say. "For the Spirit too comes to the aid of our weakness; for we do not know how to pray as we ought, but the Spirit itself intercedes with inexpressible groanings for us. And the one who searches hearts knows what is the intention of the Spirit, because it intercedes for the holy ones according to God's will" (Rom. 8:26–27). The Holy Spirit helps us in our weakness and, though we do not know how to pray as we ought, the Spirit continues His work in the world, teaching us how to pray and praying for us on our behalf.

Wisdom teaches us that true prayer is not an achievement but a gift. It does not change God but changes us. We must come to pray not giving God instructions but just reporting for duty. We must realize that the reason for prayer is not to get favors or answers from God—it is to gain perfect and complete union with our God. It is an occasion to seek to understand God and ask Him what He wants us to do, instead of just giving God instructions on what He should do for us. It is an opportunity to ask God to help us grow in virtue and love, to be inspired to live life to the fullest and follow Christ. We learn that it is the Spirit of Christ who really prays within us, and we need only to surrender to the moment, or to the Word, or to the silence, or to the agony. We learn that true prayer is the acceptance of the truth that we are loved unconditionally. In this beautiful wisdom, we learn to allow that truth to heal us of our past, to heal us of our sins, to heal us of our insufficiency, to heal us of our guilt, to heal us of our lowliness, to heal us of our brokenness, and to set us free. We learn to accept that God loves us as we are, unconditionally and forever! How incredible is that!

In order for us to become more like Jesus Christ, we must pray to become full of a passion to become like Him. We must first die to ourselves completely and wholly. We must remember that our God is a God of second chances, a God of unending mercy and love, a God who sent His only Son to die for our sins. His Son forgave the people who put Him to death—surely, He will forgive us all of our sins and offenses if we but ask for His mercy and beg for forgiveness. We must come before our God with total humility and sorrow, admit that we are sinners, beg for His forgiveness and mercy, acknowledge Him as our Lord and Savior, and promise to turn our lives around and strive to follow His commandments. Once you have done this, you will be liberated and feel an incredible flow of emotion, a lifting of an enormous weight from your shoulders. You will feel enveloped by God's loving and all-embracing arms and surrounded by His mercy and love. You will become a new person—clean and white, innocent and beautiful. It is then that you will feel yourself worthy to serve our God and others in everyone you meet and with every opportunity that is given to you. It is then that you will feel a willingness to be present to others in their needs, whether emotional or physical or spiritual or psychological.

Start and end each day with prayer and come to God as a child. Give thanks to God for all His gifts because everything you have is a gift from God. Every night before you go to sleep, review your day with God and ask God's forgiveness for all the times you fell down that day, all the times you did or said or thought the wrong thing that day, all the times you failed to do or say what you should have done or said that day. Clean the slate and ask God's help to start over the next day doing His will. Do not end your day without this because you do not know if you will see tomorrow. Ask for God's forgiveness and tell Him you are sorry. Try to repair what you can right away before the day is over. If you have stolen something, try to give it back; if you have had a fight, tell that person that you are sorry. Do the best you can every day. Remember that God is forgiving and merciful if you are sorry, and remember that God allows U-turns. He is a God of second chances— always. We must examine our hearts carefully, first to see if we have forgiven others and if we have forgiven ourselves, for how can we ask God's forgiveness if we have not forgiven others and ourselves? Remember that if you are truly sorry and really mean it with a clean heart and truly confess your sins to God, then God will forgive you. Then pray to be able to forgive those who have hurt you and forgive them as you have been forgiven.

Matthew Kelly says it beautifully, "Prayer is powerful. Prayer is essential. Prayer cuts through and clarifies. Prayer gives us vision, courage, strength, and endurance. Prayer dissolves our prejudices, banishes our narrow mindedness, and melts away our judgmental tendencies. Prayer erodes our impure motives. Prayer opens people's hearts to God and His ways" (Arroyo 2007). Pray in the silence of your heart all day. Do not have the philosophy that you will pray only when you have time—have the philosophy that all that you think and do and say is a prayer. Ask for God's help all day, talk to God all day, bring Him your burdens all day, bring Him your joys all day, and bring Him your life all day. He already knows everything about you, so you can talk to Him about anything. Know that you are nothing without God. Give Him credit for all that you do and give endless thanksgiving to Him for all that He does for you constantly. Talking to God is prayer, working for God is prayer, singing for God is prayer, and sacrificing for God is prayer. "Pray continuously; give thanks in all circumstances. For this is God's will for you in Christ Jesus" (Thes. 5:6–18).

Look at all of your unpleasant or difficult or burdensome or tiring tasks as ministries and make them a prayer. If raising your toddler tires you out completely, look at this beautiful task as a ministry. If ironing and doing laundry are unpleasant for you, look at these tasks as ministries. If cleaning the bathroom is a menial task for you, look at this as a ministry. Doing this will put the lowliest or most difficult task into perspective, and change the focus from one of drudgery to one of joy. Do all that you do for the glory of God and turn your everyday tasks into prayers.

Prayer feeds the soul and gives it strength. Just as blood is to the body, prayer is to the soul. It brings you in union with God and cleanses your heart so that you can speak to God, listen to God and hear God, and see that God in others. When your heart is clean, it is honest with God. Pray to God and ask for His strength in all that you do. Pray often and pray with utmost joy and confidence. Honestly express your emotions to God—feelings of anger, guilt, grief, etc. God can handle it. Honest praying opens the way for Got to heal our hurtful feelings and help us handle what cannot be changed. Depression thrives on repressed feelings of anger or fear or guilt or grief. Pray honestly and, many times, your honest prayers will thwart feelings of depression over things you cannot change. In response to our honest prayer, God will either change the circumstances or give us sufficient power to overcome them. God answers either the petition or the person. When the circumstances cannot be changed, God answers the person. This answer may come in different ways—maybe as peace to accept a certain situation, maybe as a calmness to relieve anxiety, maybe by patience to live or work with a person who is not willing to change, maybe through strength to persevere, etc. We must ask God for escape and encouragement. When God answers, He will give us what it takes to live with what we cannot change. Sometimes the simplest thing to do is just to give your worries to God. *I can't; God can. I think I'll let God. Let go; let God.*

You cannot get good at anything without lots of practice. You cannot get good at prayer without lots of practice. Ask God all day for opportunities to serve Him. Acknowledge God's help in all of your accomplishments. Know that, without God, you are nothing, and with God, you are everything.

The Catholic Mass has a beautiful prayer that says, "Deliver us, Lord, from every evil, and grant us peace in our day. In Your mercy, keep us free from sin and protect us in all anxiety as we wait in joyful hope for the coming of our Savior, Jesus Christ."

"And I tell you, ask and you will receive; seek and you will find; knock and the door will be opened to you. For everyone who asks, receives; and the one who seeks, finds; and to the one who knocks, the door will be opened" (Luke 11:9–10). We must always ask for God's help. We must surrender to ourselves and recognize and realize that it is not until we give our lives and problems and fears and everything we are over to God that we will be set free and things will be alright. St. Vincent de Paul tells us, "My friend, you belong to God. Let this reality color your entire existence. Give yourself up to God ceaselessly with every beat of your heart" (St. Vincent de Paul, 1580–1660). We must keep giving our worries to God in prayer unceasingly. We cannot just do it once and then think we're set for life. That would be like eating a huge meal once and thinking we'll never be hungry again. Things do not work that way. We have to eat daily to be sustained. And so it is with giving our worries, our fears, our anxieties to God. We must give these to our God consistently and repeatedly and without fail.

Pray with utmost confidence that your prayer will be heard. Whenever you feel there is a disconnect between you and your God for any reason, turn to Him immediately and ask Him to bring you rest. Never allow anything to remain which is causing or encouraging this restlessness. "Come to me, all you who are weary and burdened, and I will give you rest" (Matt. 11:28). Do not allow self-pity to creep in. Ask continuously for awareness of your God and this will be given to you. A child of God never feels the need to be made aware of the presence of their God and aware that their God answers prayer. A child of God is totally confident that God always does answer their prayers.

We are so very lucky for we are God's chosen ones, His children, and we have such easy and immediate access to God at any time and place. We have been promised that we will be refused nothing if we just ask. Many people use the adage, "God helps those who help themselves," but I have always believed that God helps those who ask for His help. We must look at prayer as a necessity and not as an option. We must ask God to teach us to pray. Prayers must become for us, as Christians, no more optional as breathing or eating or sleeping. We must look at prayer as our lifeline to God and we must look to God as the source of our very existence. So, it makes sense to be in continuous contact with that source of our life. God is as necessary in our lives as blood continually running through our blood vessels. It is in God that we breathe and move and exist. "Amen, amen I say to you, whatever you ask the Father in my name, He will give you. Until now, you have not asked anything in My name; ask and you will receive so that your joy may be complete" (John 16:23–24). "And whatever you ask in My name, I will do so that the Father may be glorified in the Son. If you ask anything of Me in My name, I will do it" (John 14:13–14). Remember that prayer is not used to change God; prayer changes us. Use prayer as an opportunity to try to understand God more instead of as an opportunity to give God His daily instructions. Approach prayer as an opportunity of growing in virtue. Pray every day for God to show you how you can become a better person that day.

Some beautiful definitions of prayer include the following:

> "Prayer is your heartbeat in tune with
>   His" (Mother Angelica).
> "Prayer is a manifestation of divine glory"
>   (St. John of Damascus, 690–749).

"Prayer is a treasure" (St. Alphonsus
     Liguori, 1696–1787).
"Prayer is the key to heaven" (St.
     Augustine, 354–430).
"Prayer is man's greatest virtue" (St. Peter
     Julian Eymard, 1811–1868).
"Prayer is a pious way of forcing God"
     (St. John Climacus, d. 649).
"Prayer is food for the soul" (Mother Angelica).
"Prayer is the bridge over temptations; and the
     death of sadness; and the token of future
     glory" (St. John Climacus, d. 649).
"Prayer is the holy water that by its
     flow makes the plants of our good
     desires grow green and flourish" (St.
     Francis de Sales, 1567–1622).
"Prayer means living in the best
     moment" (Mother Angelica).
"Prayer is a wine which makes great the heart
     of man" (St. Bernard, 1090–1153).
"Prayer is an uplifting of the heart;
     a cry of gratitude and love" (St.
     Therese of Lisieux, 1873–1897).
"Prayer is to take your failings, your
     evil tendencies, and struggle with
     them" (Mother Angelica).

Dear good and gracious God!
May we pray with expectation and confidence,
Trusting totally in Your love,
And knowing without a doubt that You will
hear us and answer us as You see fit.
And we ask this all in the most holy name
of Jesus Chris, your Son, Amen.

Intercessory Prayer

Pray at all times and on every occasion,
In the power of the Holy Spirit.
—Ephesians 6:18

Much is written about intercessory prayer and how powerful it can be. The difference between intercessory prayer and praying for yourself or for some personal gain or help is that intercessory prayer is said on behalf of or for someone else. In fact, in many instances, God makes the pouring out of His blessings on others dependent on our prayers. But it is not just praying for someone else or their needs—it is praying with the real hope and real intent and real confidence that God will answer the prayers prayed for the good of some specific other person or persons or some specific other group or groups, and that God will step in and act for the good of someone else. It is someone standing up for others before God and trusting that God will act according to His will and His timing. We can act as the intercessor of God's love for those for whom we pray because of God's unending and merciful love for us. Intercessory prayer is asking our God to benefit or bless someone other than ourselves. Jesus Christ was a prime example of an intercessor. Intercessory prayer has as its goal to build people into what God wants of them. Therefore, we should pray in such a manner as to commit everything to the gracious will of God, and let God determine whether it is conducive to His honor and His will and to the benefit of those for whom we pray (Matt. 8:1–13). We must remember that when we use intercessory prayer, we cannot fathom God's will or His purposes, or know for sure what God knows about the future. God's love quite simply has much deeper, broader, and longer work to do, and sometimes what an intercessor prays for simply cannot fit into God's plan. As an intercessor, we must pray with confidence that, whatever needs to happen will. As intercessors, we must pray that

God's will be done. This is putting our trust in God that He knows best.

When we pray as intercessors, we may find that sometimes God delays giving His answer to our prayers. It is almost as if God says to us, "I can't help you this time" or "I can't help you right now." It is not easy to persevere and continue our prayers in the confidence that He will answer our prayers. But this is exactly what our God wants and expects of us, and He totally values our trust and ongoing self-assurance that He will answer our prayers as He sees fit. This is true faith and, as such, gives glory to our God.

Intercessory prayer must start with each of us. If God's love is at work in you, you will care about others and your love of them will lead you to pray for them to the ultimate source of healing, love, mercy, strength, hope, compassion, and enlightenment. God tells us not to be afraid to approach Him and that He does not mind your acting on behalf of others—those who have strayed, those that are lost, those who are afraid, those who feel unworthy, those who have gone down the wrong path. When we pray for others, we do not pray alone, for the Holy Spirit prays with us and is leading us to pray. Intercessory prayer is prayer that is prayed to the Father, through the Son, and with the Holy Spirit. Since we are not shown what our God actually wants us to pray for as an intercessor for someone else, we must pray simply to hear the Holy Spirit and pray that God's will be done. When you pray for others, offer up to God your own talents and gifts and abilities and energy, and ask God to use these on behalf of those for whom you are praying.

Let us, because of our faith in our God, become intercessors. When we see others in pain, others suffering, others afraid, others lost, let us not hesitate a moment to allow their needs to stir our spirit of compassion and cause us to pray for them. Stop immediately and offer a prayer for them and then add these people and their intentions to your list of friends and relatives whom you pray for daily. Pray for your neighbors, pray for your enemies, pray for your leaders, pray for sinners that they may come back to Christ, pray for the sick and for the suffering, pray for the intentions of others. Pray at all times and be persistent in your prayers. We need to recognize the foolishness of living entirely for ourselves and recognize the incredible gift we have to give when we pray for others and their needs. "But I tell you this—though He won't do it as a friend, if you keep knocking long enough, he will get up and give you what you want so his reputation won't be damaged" (Luke 11:8). The qualities of a true intercessor are a Christ-like love for others, the recognition of a person's inadequacies to and need for assistance, a faithful steadfastness in prayer despite some delay in God's answer to prayer, and an absolute confidence that God hears for what we pray.

Matthew Kelly tells us that "Prayer is powerful. Pray is essential. Prayer cuts through and clarifies. Prayers gives us vision, courage, strength, and endurance. Prayer dissolves our prejudices, banishes our narrow mindedness, and melts away our judgmental tendencies, Prayer erodes our impure motives. Prayer opens people's hearts to God and His ways. Our work to share the Gospel with others should never be separated from our prayer for those people" (Kelly 2002). Anyone can pray for others and talk to God on their behalf. They can take the needs of others before God on their behalf. They should not worry about it and should pray with utmost confidence on behalf of that person. And they should pray that God's will be done. "Therefore, faith prays in such a manner that it commits everything to the gracious will of God; it lets God determine whether it is conducive to His honor and to our benefit" (Matt. 8:1–13).

Footprints in the Sand by Mark Hargrave:

One night I dreamed of walking along
        the shores of different lands.
I could tell that You were with me by
        the footprints in the sand.
As I gazed upon the heavens, I
        saw pages of my life.
It was then I realized that You
        remained there by my side.
When the clouds began to gather and
        the rains came falling down,
I looked to only find one set of
        footprints on the ground.
I said, "Lord, why did You leave me
        in the troubled times of life?
I believed that You would always walk beside
        me day and night." (Then I heard:)
"My precious child, I'd never leave you.
I have carved you on the hollow of My hand.
It's then I carried you in My arms,
When you see one set of
        footprints in the sand"
Dear Lord, will You be with me as I
        travel through the years?

Will You be there in the struggles?
      Will You wipe away the tears?
As my eyes turn toward the ocean and
      the shores of distant lands,
I'm still thinking of the single set of footprints
      in the sand. (I heard Him say:)
"My precious child, I'd never leave you.
I have carved you on the hollow of My hand.
It's then I carried you in My arms,
When you see one set of footprints
      in the sand."
Will I hear the angels singing, as
      my life comes to an end.
Oh Lord, I long to see You. Will
      You be there once again?
My eyes turn toward the heavens, along
      the path of foreign lands,
Once more, I'm thinking of the set of
      footprints in the sand. (Jesus said:)
"My precious child, I'd never leave you.
See your name carved on the
      hollow of My hand.
I'm here to carry you to your home.
You will see one set of footprints in the sand.

Try to become more astute to the needs of others and aware of their needs. If you see someone in physical or emotional or spiritual pain, start praying for them and help carry their burden. Do not worry for them; instead, pray for them with the confidence that God will hear your prayer and answer it in His way. As Jesus taught His disciples, we should pray that God's purposes be fulfilled everywhere and that His will be done, trusting in the all-knowing God that He knows best. We should pray on behalf of our loved ones and then rest in the peace of knowing that God hears our prayers and answers them in His time and in His place and according to His will. If someone asks you to pray for them, be first complete in Christ and then pray, and your prayer will be victorious. Let us face the incredible need of people "starving" for our help, perishing of hunger when there is enough spiritual bread to eat. Our own family and friends, people entrusted to us, people who are despairing, people who are in need of our prayers, those dying without hope. When we have true love for others, we must feel the spirit of intercession. "Wherefore, take unto you the whole armour of God…. Praying always with all prayer and supplication in the Spirit, and watching thereunto with all perseverance and supplication for all saints"

(Eph. 6:13, 18). Remember, "The earnest prayer of a righteous person has great power and wonderful results" (James 5:16). "Never minimize the power of the least insignificant prayer, because God hears you. And for some of you, He'd be so tickled to hear your voice at all" (Arroyo 2007).

Dear good and gracious God!
Give us the passion and love to pray
*   for the souls of others,*
May we stay restless until others are saved,
And may we, even though poor ourselves, be
*   used to make others rich in Your blessings,*
And realize always that those things we
*   cannot possibly do for others,*
Can be attained through the power
*   of intercessory prayer.*
Teach us to pray;
Teach us to recognize You in all that
*   we think and do and say;*
Teach us to acknowledge Your
*   greatness in all that we do;*
Teach us to ask You how to pray:
Teach us to never be afraid, to never avoid
*   You, to never feel unworthy;*

Teach us that You will envelop us in Your
loving arms of mercy and love always.
And we ask this all in the most holy name
of Jesus Christ, Your Son, Amen

Grace

For God so loved the world that He gave His only Son,
So that everyone who believes in Him might
not perish but might have eternal life.
—John 3:16–18

What is grace? Grace is God's abundant love for us—regardless! Grace is giving the benefit of the doubt; grace forgives and goes on with life; grace is not a reciprocal deal; grace guarantees a future, no matter what we did; grace is the glory of God; grace is greater than all of our sins; grace heals the wounds that our sins have caused; grace helps us to maintain moral balance; grace helps us to persevere in the pursuit of virtue; grace enlightens our minds to see and know which actions will help us become all God has created us to be; grace inspires us to love what is good and shun what is evil; grace is the power of God alive within us (Kelly 2002). God gives us the ability to rise up after falling and begin again. God helps us to endure the crosses He sends us.

We must take the grace that is given to us by God and pass it along to others. Jesus Christ told us to be like Him in all that we do, so we must not hoard the grace He gives to us. Instead, we must pass it on as He passes it onto us. We too must give people the benefit of the doubt, we too must show forgiveness and go on with life, we too must be kind to all, we too must overlook the faults of others, we too must show mercy to all, and we too must not hold a grudge but must let things go. Grace means being generous with our resources to those in need. It means kindness to all, it means we must overlook *everyone's* faults, it means generosity in material things, it means generosity of spirit, it means letting people in in traffic, it means helping someone move, it means making a meal for someone in need, it means taking time for others, it means cutting an elderly neighbor's grass, it means taking out the trash for the widow next door, it means visiting a shut-in or having them over for dinner, it means bringing some flowers to someone who has no family, and it means volunteering at the food pantry. Grace conquers preferences, pride, and prejudice and all other barriers to get to the heart of the problems behind those barriers. It often takes a person into risky places—risky places of the heart and mind, and risky places of the soul. But we must remember that Jesus Christ went into risky places too and died for all of us. He forgave us all, even those who drove the nails into His hands and feet, so we too must be willing to forgive EVERYONE, even if we do not think they deserve it. For we, too, are the most undeserving of offenders before Jesus Christ, and yet we were forgiven and forgiven wholeheartedly.

You must strive to become a person filled with the grace of Jesus Christ. You may, at first, think that you cannot be this person—a person with a soft side, the grace-filled "be nice to everybody" side, the "hug everybody" side, the "be kind to at least one person who is undeserving of you today" side. But through the undying and reliable grace of God, you can be this person. And our loving and grace-filled God will be with you every step of the way and will, in fact, show you the way if you but ask for His help. For our God is a God of reliability and grace—you can always count on His grace. We too must strive to become people of reliable grace. We must go out and strive to touch lives and change them. We must be people who show character in all that we do, even in the most difficult of times. We must inspire others with our unwavering strength and courage. We must strive to be an incentive for others to be good and to do good.

Grace is an ongoing conscious act of abundant and unceasing kindness, no matter what, even to the most undeserving of offenders and sinners. It should be given to everyone, without exception, even to those least deserving. Our God is slow to anger—we must be also. That is the mark of reliable grace. Grace is giving people a second chance. Grace is giving people space and not demanding more of them than we demand of ourselves. It seems we always want others to give us space, but we are not willing to do the same for others. We need to work on that. We must expect much of ourselves before we expect much of others. We must remove the log from our own eye before we attempt to remove the splinter from the eye of another. Grace is not operating under a double standard.

Grace is giving people the benefit of the doubt. Grace takes the spotlight off of our needs and focuses it on the needs of others, especially on the needs of the poor and helpless and undeserving. Grace never asks for anything in return. It should not be, "I'll cut your grass if you agree to pay me," or "I'll give you something to eat if you wash my car." No, it should be given away unconditionally, requiring nothing in return. Grace forgives and forgets and goes on with life. It refuses to be stuck in a world of past offenses. Grace forgives what happened yesterday or last week or last month or last year, and does not bring it up again—EVER! "As the heavens tower over the earth, so God's love towers over the faithful. As far as the east is from the west, so far have our sins been removed from us" (Psalm 103:11–12).

Grace forgives those who have offended us as we have always been and continually are forgiven by our God. Grace is not always fair, just as our God is not always fair—thank God! Think about it—would it not be awful if our God treated us and forgave us in the same measure as we have treated Him? What a totally merciful and compassionate God we have! Grace guarantees us that we will always have a future and a chance after we have sinned—even in the most horrible of ways. How totally awesome and comforting is that?

St. Paul tells us to "put to death therefore what is earthly in you: immorality, impurity...evil desires, and covetousness" (Col. 3:5). Let us pray now that we can die to ourselves so that we too can start to become like our God—full of reliable grace in all that we do. Let us pray that we might strive to be portals of grace to all.

God elevates us by His grace to places we cannot imagine exist. And in so doing, He continually beckons us to ascend higher and higher spiritually through insight into our characters. Although God purifies us by His grace, we must continuously strive to keep our inner sanctuary right with God so that we will be able to keep pure our thoughts and actions with the people with whom we come into contact and those with other points of view. Grace is the strength we need to keep going in the direction of spirituality in all that we do. It is God's gentle molding of us into the creatures He wants us to be. It is God's love that is unending and will continue to flow into us. Grace is the overflowing favor of God that you can always count on to be there to draw upon in your moments of need. "One of the greatest proofs that you are drawing on the grace of God is that you can be humiliated without manifesting the slightest trace of anything but His grace" (Chambers 1963). If we are going to live as disciples of Jesus Christ, we must know that God saves men by His sovereign grace through the atonement of Jesus Christ. "If we obey the Spirit of God and practice in our physical life what God has put in us by His Spirit, then when the crisis comes, we shall find that our own nature, as well as the grace of our God, will stand by us" (Chambers 1963).

Dear good and gracious God!
Again we come before You in humility and shame,
  in need of Your forgiveness and mercy.
There are so many times that we have failed
  to extend Your grace to others;
So many times that we have kept
  Your grace to ourselves,
Unwilling to forgive and forget;
So many times that we have fallen and sinned,
Forgetting to ask for Your grace and help.
Help us to recognize opportunities to share
  Your grace with those around us,
With those we do not like,
With those we find undeserving,
With those who anger us.
We are broken and in need of Your healing.
Show us Your love and forgiveness and
  mercy as You do constantly.

*Fill us with Your grace and healing, and
help us to extend Your grace to all.
We ask this all in the most holy name of
Jesus Christ, Your Son, amen.*

Charity

And when he had called the people
unto him with his disciples also,
He said unto them,
"Whosoever will come after me,
Let him deny himself and take up
his cross and follow me."
—Mark 8:34–37

"Charity is that with which no man is lost, and without which no man is saved" (St. Robert Bellarmine, 1542–1621). So much of our life gets lost in the pursuit of things we think are important. We trade our time for that which does not matter. We trade our energy for gains never realized. We trade our hopes for what winds up as wrecked dreams. We must learn to focus our lives and do only those things which really matter, and remember that what matters most will ultimately be what God says about our lives—what we did on earth to create our eternal rather than our earthly legacy. Jesus tells us, "If any of you wants to be my follower, you must put aside your selfish ambition, shoulder your cross and follow me. If you try to keep your life for yourself, you will lose it. But if you give up your life for my sake and for the sake of the Good News, you will find true life." (Matt. 16:24-26). "And how do you benefit if you gain the whole world but lose your own soul in the process? Is anything worth more than your soul? If a person is ashamed of me and my message in these adulterous and sinful days, I, the Son of Man, will be ashamed of that person when I return in the glory of my Father with the holy angels" (Mark 8:36-38). As Matthew Kelly so poignantly puts it, "For the most part, we are too busy doing just about everything, that means just about nothing, to just about nobody, just about anywhere…and will mean even less to anyone a hundred years from now!" (Kelly 1999). We must live in such a way that when we stand before our God and He asks us what we did with the gifts He gave us—our talents, our abilities, our possessions—we will be able to say that we used them wisely and for His purposes instead of our own.

We have become stubborn and self-serving—sometimes quite lost in a limited vision of only our own space and time. Sometimes we can hardly hear words of truth anymore because we simply want to hear just our own. Long ago, Christ sent this warning, "If you were blind, you would have no guilt; but now that you see, we see; your guilt remains" (John 9:41). "You shall indeed hear but never understand, and you shall indeed see but never perceive. For this people's heart has grown dull, and their ears are heavy of hearing, and their eyes have closed, lest they should perceive with their eyes, and hear with their ears, and understand with their heart" (Matt. 13:14–15).

We are taught that we must reach out to our neighbor in need, no matter who our neighbor might be, for this is what constitutes true charity that is pleasing to our God. It is our moral and ethical duty to respond to those who suffer because of injustice, those who struggle to get by, those who live in fear, those who are oppressed, those who are weak, those who cannot fight back on their own, those who cannot make it on their own, those who need help. *"We must love our neighbor as being made in the image of*

God and as a subject of His love" (St. Vincent de Paul, 1580–1660). The most damaging aspect of contemporary living is short-term thinking. "To make the most of your life, you must keep the vision of eternity closely in your mind, and the value of it in your heart" (Warren 2008).

Here is what the church has to say about our reaching out to others: "Today, there is an inescapable duty to make ourselves the neighbor of every man, no matter who he is, and if we meet him, to come to his aid in a way, whether he is an aged person abandoned by all, a foreign worker despised without reason, a refugee, an illegitimate child wrongly suffering for a sin he did not commit, or a starving human being who awakens our conscience by calling to mind the words of Christ—'as you did to one of the least of these, my brethren, you did it to me'" (John 25:40; VC, GS, No. 27). "We ought to respect the image of God in everyone. It is there" (Blessed Raphaela Mary, 1850–1925).

Certainly, all of these demeaning conditions need to be responded to by acts of Christian charity by loving one another as our Lord has commanded. We are surrounded by people in need, people who we can assist and love, people we must not judge but simply help. To not help our brother or sister in need simply pays lip service to our faith instead of living our faith as an act of charity toward God and our neighbor. We must *walk the walk* and not just *talk the talk*. "Charity knows no bounds of race, colour, creed or distance. The parable of the Good Samaritan proclaims that everyone is our neighbour. The tiny orphan wandering and wailing through some evil smelling Honk Kong slum, the blind beggar squatting awkwardly on a teeming Bombay sidewalk, unkept and unheeded—or nearer home, the sick, the aged, the unemployed; all need our prayers or alms or both. For charity is the great white dividing line between the children of God and the children of men" (Johnston, *Voice of the Saints*, 27–28).

The Magesterium of the Catholic Church says it very clearly: "Wherever men are to be found who are in want of food and drink, of clothing, housing, medicine, work, education, the means necessary for leading a truly human life; wherever there are men racked by misfortune or illness, men suffering exile or imprisonment, Christian charity should go in search of them and find them out, comfort them with devoted care and give them the help that will release their needs" (VC, AA, No. 8).

It is so very easy to help those whom we like— our friends, our neighbors, our relatives—and, certainly, acts of kindness toward these are good and deserve merit. But the true test of our faith and charity comes when our help is given to those we detest, to those of whom we do not approve, to those we feel are unworthy of our help, to those we feel deserve to be in the state in which they are. "For if you love those who love you, what reward have you?" (Matt. 5:46). "The sun rises on the evil and on the good, and God sends rain on the just and the unjust" (Matt. 5:44). And this is a command that we must take very seriously. God tells us that in His kingdom, he that is greatest is the servant of all. The greatest of all saints is not preaching the Gospel of Christ, but washing the feet of disciples, i.e., doing things that do not count in the eyes of men but count immensely in the kingdom of God. "Love the poor tenderly, regarding them as your masters and yourselves as their servants" (St. John of God, 1495–1550). God does not merely suggest this to us—He commands it. He does not make it an option according to our preferences or favoritism. Each human being should be looked upon by his neighbor (without any exception) as another self, bearing in mind above all his life and the means necessary for living it in a dignified way, "lest he follow the example of the rich man who ignored Lazarus, the poor man" (Luke 16:1–31; VC, GS, No.

27). "We must above all show charity to our enemies. Do good to those that hate you" (Matthew 44). 'By this you may know that a man is a true Christian, if he seeks to do good to those who wish him evil" (St. Alphonsus Liguori, 1696–1787).

Peter, when God asked him if he loved Him, kept saying, "Yes, Lord, I love you." "Then feed my lambs," God said. Again God asked Peter, "Do you love me?" and again Peter says, "Yes, Lord, I love you." "Then tend my sheep," God said. A third time, God asked Peter, "Do you love me?" and again Peter said, "Yes, Lord, I love you." And a third time, God said, "Then feed my sheep." God's question to Peter hurt Peter very much until Peter finally got it—God was telling him to not just talk the talk but to walk the walk. *If you love Me, then feed My sheep. Don't just tell Me how much you love Me; don't just talk about how great I am—feed My sheep"* (John 21:15–17). Love is complete and simple obedience to our God without excuses, without exception, without watering down, and without escape clauses. God's sheep are many and come in all shapes and sizes, but we have no business to choose which sheep to feed. If we love God, we will feed His sheep—one and all.

We must learn to distinguish between the mistake made or the sin committed by a person (which must always be rejected), and the person who makes the mistake or commits the sin, who never loses his dignity as a person even though he sins or makes a mistake. We must remember that God alone is the judge who knows a person's heart, and that we are not to pass judgment on the inner guilt of others. We must learn to love the sinner and hate the sin. It is God's grace that allows us to recognize the difference between the sin and the sinner, separating out the sin but still loving the sinner, and showing charity toward him.

Christ teaches us to forgive injury and to forgive everyone—even our enemies. "But I say to you, love your enemies, do good to them that hate you; and pray for those who persecute and calumniate you" (Matt. 5:43–44).

Pope Paul VI acknowledged our duty as good Christians to help others to improve their quality of life. He said, "The members of mankind share the same basic rights and duties, as well as the same supernatural destiny. Within a country which belongs to each one, all should be equal before the law, find equal admittance to economic, civic and social life, and benefit from a fair sharing of the nation's riches" (Pope Paul VI, Apostolic Letter Octogenesima Adveniens, 1971). How can we all, in a practical manner, carry our share of the burden? One way is to change our attitudes concerning our material possessions. Those of us who live in wealth and overabundance need to learn to strip ourselves of the material things we do not need and give to those in need who cry out for our mercy and love. We must learn to separate our desires from our needs, and learn that money can lead to greed. Money in and of itself is not evil, but it is in the way we use it (or hoard it) that can make us sin against our neighbor. "Wealth ill becomes the mean man; and to the miser, of what use is gold? What he denies himself, he collects for others and, in his possessions, a stranger will revel. To whom will he be generous who is stingy with himself, and does not enjoy what is his own? None is stingier than he who is stingy with himself; he punishes his own miserliness. If ever he is generous, it is by mistake; and in the end, he displays his greed. In the miser's opinion, his share is too small; he refuses his neighbor and brings ruin on himself" (Sirach 14:3–9).

We should also take heed and follow the advice of Sirach when he tells us: "Nevertheless, be patient with a man in humble circumstances, and do not make him wait for your alms. Help a poor man for the commandment's sake and, because of his need, do not send him away empty" (Sirach 29:8–9).

We cannot say that we love God if we do not show a corresponding charity toward our neighbors, one and all. We are told to "do for one another" (1 Cor. 12:25). Jesus quite explicitly commands that in order to serve Him, we must follow Him (John 12:26). And He tells us, "if any man would come after Me, let him deny himself and take up his cross and follow Me" (Luke 9:23). Luke 9:23 opens with the words, *"And He said to all."* He wasn't just talking to His friends, His disciples, His apostles—He was talking to *all* of us. In order to please our God, there are many sacrifices and sufferings that He accepts from us if done in a true spirit of charity and love. He tells us to "beware of practicing your piety before men in order to be seen by them...But when you give alms, do not let your left hand know what your right is doing, so that your alms may be in secret. And your Father, who sees in secret, will reward you" (Matt. 6:1; 3–4). "You are those who justify yourselves before men, but God knows your hearts; for what is exalted among men is an abomination in the sight of God" (Luke 16:15). We must strive to follow the will of God concerning those for whom we sacrifice. If we sacrifice only what *we* choose or in the manner that *we* choose, we put our own will before the will of God. "But seek first His kingdom and His righteousness, and all these things shall be yours as well" (Matt. 7:21). "Not everyone who says to Me, 'Lord, Lord' shall enter the kingdom of heaven, but he who does the will of the Father who is in heaven" (Matt. 7:21).

Jesus tells us, "If anyone would be first, he must be last of all and servant of all" (Matt. 9:35). He strives for the absolute necessity of being humble and tells us that to be humble is to serve each other and to care for each other's needs. "Even as the Son of man came not to be served, but to serve, and to give His life as a ransom for many" (Matt. 20:28). Everyone on the path to perfection must serve each other (Matt. 10:43), for in so doing, we are *really* serving the Lord. "Truly I say to you, as you did it to one of the least of My brethren, you did it to Me" (Matt. 25:40).

Above all, Jesus teaches us to sacrifice and serve from the depths of our hearts, and not for public praise and acknowledgement. And He teaches us that "everyone to whom much is given, of him much will be required; and of him to whom much is entrusted, more will be demanded of the person entrusted with more" (Luke 12:48). He tells us, "If anyone serves Me, he must follow Me; and where I am, there shall

My servant be" (John 12:26). Good deeds and generosity are pleasing to our God (Heb. 13:16).

St. John assures us, through the words of our Lord, that it is through true service to others that we can best express the spirit of our faith. He tells us that love ensures our sacrifices for each other, not just by prayer or by talking about it, but also through positive action that leads to a wholeness of life. Sacrifice and suffering for others is simply not enough. Faith without action is dead. Jesus Himself not only suffered for our sakes, but served others in time of need. "You call me teacher and Lord; and you are right, for so I am. If I then, your Lord and teacher, have washed your feet, you also ought to wash one another's feet. For I have given you an example that you also should do as I have done to you" (John 13:13–15). Jesus indicates that our motive for service to one another must be selfless love. Doing good works are visible signs that express our faith to others. These good works cause us to be a light that shines for the world to see—a sign of Christ's presence among us. "If I am not doing the works of My Father, then do not believe me; but if I do them, even though you do not believe Me, believe the works, that you may know and understand that the Father is not Me and I am not the father" (John 10:37–38).

Dear good and gracious God!
Let us make a difference in the world.
Let us be the hands of Christ,
Reaching out to those in need.
Let us be the face of God for all to see,
The love of God in you and me.
Let us be the spirit of hope,
Not to be hidden but seen.
We ask this all in the most holy name of
Jesus Christ, Your Son, Amen.

Barriers to Serving Others

We acknowledge God's freedom and
grace though we are unworthy.
The Lord has made us His own in Christ.
God has chosen us as His servants
for the sake of the world.
And destined us to be His daughters and sons,
Giving us love and life,
Calling us to worship and honor Him.
—Agar

Through prayer, we are made holy and God's mercy and power begin to work in us and help us to overcome the strongholds in our lives that separate us from Him, one by one, through God's grace working in us. In his last public teaching, Jesus describes the final judgment as being based solely and completely on behavioral responses to internalized compassion. And Jesus makes it quite clear that those who DO express universal compassion in behavioral action WILL BE SAVED, and that those who do not will NOT be saved. Period. There is no other qualification (Matt. 25:31–45). Mother Teresa juxtaposed Matthew's two messages (the *great commandment* and that what we do to *the least of these* is done to God) to theorize that whatever our actions are toward *the least of these* are actually done to God. She asserted that we fulfill the first commandment by obedience to the second, which was the motivation for her to search and find the ultimate *least of these* in the world and to serve them as if she was serving God.

There are many things that make us feel unworthy to serve others—things in our past or present life that act as barriers to serving others, such as anger, feeling unworthy in the eyes of God, the inability to forgive others or ourselves, shame, fear, lack of trust in the mercy of God, etc. Many people feel totally lost, unworthy of God's love, unable to be forgiven for their past sins, or unable to get over some past offense, literally stuck in their world of mediocrity.

If you are constantly replaying over and over in your brain the time that person made you mad or hurt you, the time that teacher made you feel stupid, the time your boyfriend or girlfriend cheated on you, the time that employer did not pay you enough, the times your mother was not the mother she should have been to you, the time that person ruined your reputation, the times you sinned against God, the times you were unfaithful to God's word—if you are stuck in the world of past sins, you need to be liberated before you will be able to serve others. Mother Teresa said it beautifully—"I know God will not give me anything I can't handle; I just wish He wouldn't trust me so much." Her barriers to do God's will were incredible, yet she walked in faith and in total trust, and the barriers went away.

If you are not moved, but instead even a little bit irritated, at the huge unemployment crisis you see around you and just want to yell out that anyone who really *wants* to work *could*, you must listen to the word of God.

If you are one of those people who hears and reads about the worldwide AIDS crisis, especially in Africa where there may literally be countries that will be completely wiped out within ten years because of one of the worst, if not *the* worst, curses in all of human history, and just brushes it aside or changes channels; or if the fact that millions and millions of orphans due to AIDS are living in Africa alone does not interest you in the least, or does not make you even give a thought to what Jesus Christ would do in the face of such an unthinkable tragedy, you need to listen to the word of God.

If you are a person who is never quite satisfied, who feels the world owes you, who feels that you're better than others, who has an attitude that rules apply to others but not to you, who feels it's okay to adjust the commandments to your liking, who feels it's okay to judge others, who has their ego stroked by pointing out the faults of others, you need to listen to the word of God.

If you are a person who feels they need to start a new journey in their lives—a journey to help you become the better person you know you can become, a journey of wanting to be more like Jesus Christ, a journey to help you radiate Jesus Christ in your life, a person who others will look at and see Jesus Christ through—then you need to listen to the word of God.

We must all realize that the journey to God may be a difficult one, a long one, a trying one, one filled with worlds of doubt, one filled with challenges and fears. Yet, He tells us that His yoke is light, so that even if it is heavy, if it is with Him, it will be light. If not with Him, it is much heavier. Yet, it will be a journey that will bring us closer and closer to becoming the better person we know we can become, a journey that will make us more like Jesus Christ than we were a year ago or a month ago or even a day ago. It will not be until we have started this journey that we will be able to answer the call to fulfill the challenges we were put on this earth to fulfill, and to answer the call to serve that each one of us was placed on this earth to answer. We must remember that being brave does not mean we do not feel afraid. It means doing the right thing *in spite* of feeling afraid. "Commit your way to the Lord; trust that God will act and make your integrity shine like the dawn, your vindication like noonday" (Psalms 37:5–6).

Dear good and gracious God!
We once more stand before You,
Humbled by Your mercy and forgiveness
for all of our brokenness;
By your unconditional love and
kindness to us, as sinners.
We struggle every day to recommit
ourselves to You and Your will,

And we fall every day in that struggle.
Help us once again to continue to get
  up and recommit ourselves;
Help us to forgive ourselves;
Help us to feel Your unconditional
  love and mercy;
And help us never to stop trying to be
  all that we can become.
We ask this all in the most holy name of
  Jesus Christ, Your Son, Amen.

Truth

No harm befalls the just,
But the wicked are overwhelmed with misfortune.
Lying lips are an abomination to the Lord,
But those who are truthful are His delight.
—Proverbs 12:21–22

God wants us to learn how to "reason in faith" by taking the truths He has revealed to us and applying them to our own philosophy of life and to the decisions we make every day. Integrity can be defined as not merely talking the talk, but walking the walk. If we say that we will do something, it is very important that we do it. That is true integrity.

Every spiritual and religious path has truth. When we look deeply into all paths, we find only one truth—that we are all one, a part of our Creator that is love.

Strive to be a person of truth at all times—a person who is always honest, always authentic, always the real deal. This is certainly a tall order—one not easy to achieve and maintain—and most people will fall and fail pretty much daily and will have to start over many times and recommit over and over again. Strive always to tell the truth, to be honest in whatever you say and do, to be brave enough to not let people get away with doing and saying things you know are wrong or prejudiced or dishonest. Make sure that no one pays back wrong for wrong, but always try to be kind to each other. Warn those who are idle, encourage the timid, help the weak, and be patient with everyone. Learn to be honest with yourself and become a person of reliable grace and a person slow to anger, as is your God. Strive to balance the grace-filled side of yourself with the side of truth. Strive to start every day fresh, and strive anew each day to be a person that treats others as you wish to be treated—not as you think they should be treated but as you wish to be treated. Strive always to be a person who is fair to all—not just those people that you feel are deserving. Strive always to be a person who gives everyone a second chance—not just those people you like. Be a person who does not judge others—leave that to a higher power. Be a person who walks a mile in everyone else's shoes. Recognize that it will not be easy to always be a person of truth, and that we all fall over and over again. It is said that the difference between a saint and an ordinary person is that the saint keeps getting up over and over every time he or she falls and starts over. We too must strive to keep getting up and starting over.

It is impossible to realize one's inner truth unless the ego dies. The "ego is the greatest obstacle on your path toward the truth" (Shri Mataji Nirmala Devi). Edgar Cayce said we should "seek first, then, within self, as to what is thy ideal. Hold fast, thou, to that strength as thou perceived that prompted the hearts and minds and bodies of those that served their fellow man without seeking for self-glorification. And with thy ideal set in the spiritual things, ye may find and ye will know the truth that was in Him. For the truth shall indeed make you free, when ye come to the understanding of same as ye apply it in thy relations to thy fellow man" (877–1).

We must realize that very few of us will ever be authorities on the truth. But we should strive always and ask for God's help to become Christ-conscious.

Our spiritual journey is one of unending learning and purification and humility. We must seek always and listen carefully to hear Christ speaking to us. We must open our hearts to the word of God and pray for our ears to be opened to hear the word of God. It is only through devotion to our God that we will come to recognize the absolute truth. True devotion is the unbroken receptivity to truth. We must always be students of truth and not just followers. We must be gentle and kind to ourselves without becoming discouraged or disheartened, and without giving up. We must trust our spiritual path and trust that we are on the path upon which God wishes us to be. Be patient on this spiritual path to truth. Just as one cannot learn a new language or algebra quickly, it also takes time for spiritual growth and truth.

As Jack Kornfield quotes in his book *A Path with Heart*, from Carlos Castaneda, "Look at every path closely and deliberately. Try it as many times as you think necessary. Then ask yourself and yourself alone one question…Does this path have a heart? If it does, the path is good. If it doesn't, then it is of no use" (Kornfield 1974).

There are many who simply procrastinate in their search for the truth, never willing to put forth the effort and commitment necessary to really find it. But "the modern faddish idea that we can always keep all our options open and so never need commit ourselves to anything is one of the greatest and most dangerous delusions of our culture, and one of ego's most effective ways of sabotaging our spiritual search" (Rinpoche 1992).

If you know anything about the Old Testament, you know that even God sometimes came across as an angry, revengeful, "come down hard on sinners" God. He was known by the people of the Old Testament as a God of faithfulness, reliable grace, and truth. The story of Jonah and the whale proves this point. Most people think that Jonah at first ran from God's command to go to Nineveh—a violent and evil place—because he was terrified of what would happen to him there if he went there and started telling the people to clean up their act. But this is not why he ran away at all. He actually tells God in chapter 4 of Jonah, in essence, "Do You want to know, God, why I didn't want to go to Nineveh in the first place and ran away when you told me go? Because I know that You are a good and merciful and forgiving God, willing to forgive those who are sorry for their sins and repent, and I didn't want these people to be forgiven of their sins." And in many ways, we have the same problem as Jonah. We know what kind of

God our God is, and we do not want to be the person to help certain people in our lives that we think are undeserving to be forgiven. God was merciful, not only to the people of Nineveh, but also to Jonah. Instead of being really angry at Jonah and freaking out, our God gently brought him back to the truth and persuaded him to do His will because our God is a God of second chances.

We must be true to ourselves and admit that there are some people whom we do not want to help, some people we do not think are deserving of God's love and mercy, some people with whom we are angry, some people who have made us so mad that we do not want them to reap the benefits of God's warmth and love. Ask for God to reveal Himself to you for He says, "I am the way and the truth and the life. No one comes to the Father except through me" (John 14:6). "He who believes in me will live, even though he dies. And whoever believes in me will never die" (John 11:25–26). Ask for this for yourself and for all people, especially those most in need. Ask God to reveal to you the absolute truth. Do not ever accept something as truth just because someone says it is true. Read what is said through the eyes of divine discerning intelligence and ask for God's wisdom within your heart to allow you to clearly understand only the truth. "At the very outset, we have to understand that we cannot create truth, we cannot organize truth. Truth is, was and will be. We cannot cheat truth. We have to reach that point to serve it. It is not a mental achievement. It is not a concept. We cannot change it. Where the seekers of truth are misled, the results have been disastrous" (Shri Mataji Nirmala Devi).

"Truth enlightens man's intelligence and shapes his freedom, leading him to know and love God" (Pope John Paul II, 1993 Encyclical Letter, Veritatis Splendor). The truth of God "will never waver. God's ways will never alter. He will always hate sin and love sinners, despise the proud and exalt the humble. He will always convict the evildoer and comfort the heavy-hearted. He never changes direction midstream, recalibrates the course mid-way home, or amends the heavenly constitution. God will always be the same" (Lucado 2004). *"Jesus Christ is the same yesterday, today and tomorrow"* (Heb. 13:8).

> *Dear good and gracious God!*
> *Show us the truth and lead us in truth.*
> *Let us recognize Your words and*
>   *understand Your teachings.*

Teach us to discern that which we hear
and teach that which You teach.
Bring the Holy Spirit into our lives to
open our ears and our hearts.
And give us the gift to pass Your truths
onto those who are open to them.
We ask this all in the most holy name of
Jesus Christ, Your Son, Amen.

Virtue

Amen, I say to you, unless you turn
and become like children,
You will not enter the kingdom of heaven.
—Matthew 18:2–9

V *irtue* is defined as *"general moral excellence; right action and thinking; goodness or morality."* We can turn into better persons only through living a virtuous life. We are not born with the quality of virtue. It is something we must learn and practice without fail over and over again. As Matthew Kelly says, "The great fallacy of the lukewarm moral life is to believe that our sole responsibility is to eliminate vice from our lives. In the absence of a sincere and focused effort to grow in virtue, vice will creep into our lives unawares in the form of a hundred different self-destructive habits" (Kelly 2002). One can never be truly happy unless we focus on becoming a virtuous person in all that we do. There are seven virtues that the church claims make up the foundation of a moral life. These virtues are the *supernatural virtues* of faith, hope and love, and *the four cardinal virtues* of prudence, justice, temperance and fortitude. "The supernatural virtues free us from self-centeredness and protect us from the ultimate vice—pride. The cardinal virtues...allow us to acquire the self-mastery necessary to make us free and capable of love" (Kelly 2002). We must remember that there is no partiality with God. He expects us all to be virtuous, and for all those times that we fail in this endeavor, we will be held accountable and must face consequences. The road to virtue is well-marked with many road signs. If we choose to ignore those road signs, or choose to travel the wrong road, there will be consequences at the end of the road. Strive to look for and follow God's road signs and we will come to the end of our lives with God saying to us, "Well done, my good and faithful servant. You have run the good race, you have fought the good fight, you have kept the faith" (2 Tim. 4–7, New American Bible).

Remember, there is no partiality with God. It is not those who hear the law and know the law and yet choose to ignore or modify it that will be found just in the sight of God; rather, those that observe and follow and teach the law will be justified. In our world today, there are three things that seem to almost totally dominate us and certainly entice us—the media, money, and the physical desire for things we do not possess. These three things can chip away at us and gradually destroy us, corrupting our minds by promoting self-centeredness. They can put us in a sheepishly quiet position to speak out against those things we know in our conscience and hearts to be wrong. Virtue can be heroic in such times and requires us to arise from our slumber and speak out against injustice, abortion, abuse. Brother Joseph (José) Munoz-Cortez before his death asked: "Why is there so little evidence among us of heroic virtue?... Since the hope arises to be a confessor, we should not hesitate. If we lose our earthly life, we gain a heavenly one. We should not fear death for Christ." Speak out; be a person of heroic virtue; show your Christian values and beliefs. Do not laugh at sin and do not endorse values you know to be wrong.

If you can keep your head when all about you
Are losing theirs and blaming it on you,
If you can trust yourself when all men doubt you,
But make allowance for their doubting too,
If you can wait and not be tired by waiting,
Or being lied about, don't deal in lies,
Or being hated, don't give way to hating,
And yet don't look too good, nor talk too wise;
If you can dream—and not make
      dreams your master,
If you can think—and not make
      thoughts your arm;
If you can meet with Triumph and Disaster
And treat those two imposters just the same;
If you can bear to hear the truth you've spoken
Twisted by knaves to make a trap for fools,
Or watch the things you gave your life to, broken,
And stoop and build 'em up with worn-out tools;
If you can make one heap of all your winnings
And risk it all on one turn of pitch-and-toss,
And lose, and start again at your beginnings
And never breathe a word about your loss;
If you can force your heart and nerve and sinew
To serve your turn long after they are gone,
And so hold on when there is nothing in you
Except the Will which says to them: "Hold on!"

If you can talk with crowds and keep your virtue,
Or walk with kings—nor lose the common touch,
If neither foes nor loving friends can hurt you;
If all men count with you, but none too much,
If you can fill the unforgiving minute
With sixty seconds' worth of distance run,
Yours is the Earth and everything that's in it,
And—which is more—you'll be a Man,
my son! (Rudyard Kipling)

Dear good and gracious God!
Again we come before you with
praise and thanksgiving,
Asking for Your gifts of the Holy Spirit,
So that we can walk in Your light
and hold our heads high,
So that we can know right from wrong
and stand up for right.
So that we dare to stand up for justice
even in light of evil.
So that our paths are well lit and
our direction clear.
So that we strive always to make our
way to You, no matter what.

So that we have the grace to run the
race and keep the faith.
We ask this all in the most Holy Name of
Jesus Christ, Your Son, Amen.

Becoming a Hero

"Come, O blessed of My Father,
Inherit the kingdom prepared for you
from the foundation of the world;
—Matthew 25:34–40

S trive to be a person like Mother Teresa who served the poorest of the poor, regardless of how or why they were in that state, and served them with absolute kindness and dignity and respect. She was a true hero—someone who took on responsibility without ever complaining, someone who spoke kindly to all, someone who was always fair, and someone who endured patiently and with utmost faith in God. She faced every day with simple courage and faith and persisted in the things that really mattered. She never judged, never asked why someone was in the condition they were in, never preached, never scolded, never showed disgust. She simply loved and served and gave dignity to all, and she was a representative of Christ to all. We too must strive to become true heroes and a representative of Christ to all. "In this life, we cannot do great things; we can only do small things with great love….At the end of our lives, we will not be judged by how many diplomas we have received, how much money we have made, or how many great things we have done. We will be judged by 'I was hungry and you gave me to eat, I was naked and you clothed me, and I was homeless and you took me in'" (Mother Teresa). Mother Teresa walked a simple path—one that consisted of silence to hear the word of God, unceasing prayer, a deep and unwavering faith in her God, unconditional love for all, joyful service to the poorest of the poor, and peace to all. As Mother Teresa said, "The fruit of silence is prayer, the fruit of prayer is faith, the fruit of faith is love, the fruit of love is service, and the fruit of service is peace." She had a simple philosophy—all human life is precious to God with no exceptions. She looked at those she served as *Christ in the distressing disguise of the poorest of the poor.* She said, "I see God in every human being. When I wash the leper's wounds, I feel I am nursing the Lord Himself." To her, every work of love done with a loving heart always brings a person closer to their God. It is through the silence of the heart that God speaks. We cannot hear God if we are not completely silent and open to His word. We must totally empty ourselves by being completely still and open to His word so that God can speak to us. As Matthew Kelly says, "Noise is the mouthpiece of the world. Silence is the mouthpiece of God. It is in the classroom of silence that God bestows His wisdom on men and women" (Kelly 1999).

Begin to think to yourself how you can become the better person you know you can become, and strive to do whatever it takes every day to become that person. Practice, practice, practice those things that will help you in this endeavor. The gifts you need to do this are the gifts of the Holy Spirit—humility and wisdom and meekness and brotherly love and endurance and strength and courage. Learn and practice self-discipline. Do without when you can and learn to separate needs from wants. Learn and practice unconditional love. To do this, you must overcome the barriers of doubt, anxiety, fear, worry, etc. Unconditional love is about acceptance and compassion and forgiveness and nonjudgment of others. Learn to separate yourself from the outcome of your actions. Be involved but do not fall apart if the outcome is not what you had hoped for or imagined. Many times, you will be judged harshly for your actions; you may be ridiculed for your acts of kindness; you may be made fun of for your unconditional love. But be a person who strives always to love as He loves, gives as He gives, rescues as He rescues, forgives as He forgives, serves as He serves, and shows mercy as He shows mercy. Strive to be holy in all that you do.

And He began to teach them saying:

Blessed are the poor in spirit, for theirs
is the kingdom of heaven.
Blessed are they who mourn, for
they will be comforted.
Blessed are the meek, for they will
inherit the land.
Blessed are they who hunger and
thirst for righteousness,
For they will be satisfied.
Blessed are the merciful, for they
will be shown mercy.
Blessed are the clean of heart, for
they will see God.

Blessed are the peacemakers, for they
will be called children of God.
Blessed are they who are persecuted for
the sake of righteousness, for theirs
is the kingdom of heaven.
Blessed are you when they insult you and
persecute you and utter every kind
of evil against you because of me.
Rejoice and be glad, for your reward will be
great in heaven. (Matt. 5:3–11)

In one of Mother Teresa's orphanages in India is the following quote:

People are often unreasonable, illogical, and
self-centered; Forgive them anyway.
If you are kind, people may accuse you of selfish,
ulterior motives; Be kind anyway.
If you are successful, you will win some false
friends and true enemies; Succeed anyway.
If you are honest and frank, people may
cheat you; Be honest and frank anyway.
What you spend years building, someone could
destroy overnight; Build anyway.
If you find serenity and happiness, they
may be jealous; Be happy anyway.

The good you do today, people will often
forget tomorrow; Do good anyway.
Give the world the best you have, and
it may never be enough; Give the
world the best you've got anyway.
You see, in the final analysis, it is
between you and God; It was never
between you and them anyway.

The Catholic Church has a list of seven corporal works of mercy and seven spiritual works of mercy. Learn them and practice them:

The Corporal Works of Mercy:
- feed the hungry
- give drink to the thirsty
- clothe the naked
- visit the imprisoned
- shelter the homeless
- visit the sick
- bury the dead

The Spiritual Works of Mercy:
- admonish the sinner
- instruct the ignorant
- counsel the doubtful

- comfort the sorrowful
- bear wrongs patiently
- forgive all injuries
- pray for the living and the dead

John Wesley has a wonderful quote:

> *Do all the good you can,*
> *Be all the means you can;*
> *In all the ways you can,*
> *In all the places you can,*
> *At all the times you can,*
> *To all the people you can,*
> *As long as ever you can.*

Be a hero and do not ever be ashamed of it. Meet your maker at the end of your life and be worthy so that He says to you, "Well done, thou good and faithful servant" (Matt. 25:21).

> *Dear good and gracious God!*
> *Help us to become heroes,*
> *To not be afraid to take risks,*
> *To not worry about the consequences of our risks;*
> *To not be afraid of what people may*
>   *say about our heroic acts;*

To not hesitate out of fear to do what is good.
And to be faithful servants until the end.
We ask this all in the most holy name of
Jesus Christ, Your Son, Amen.

Need for God

The Lord is my light and my
salvation; whom do I fear?
The Lord is my life's refuge; of whom am I afraid?
—Psalm 27:1

J oseph Stowell tells us that *the kingdom is not a field of wimps. We're called to be what? Soldiers for Him.* Before we can become a servant of God, we must realize and admit how much we need God. That is not to say that we should not be independent and self-confident. But, we must never assume or say that we do not need God and say to ourselves and others that we are totally self-reliant, nor should we say that everything we have is there because we have worked hard for it. We must not pretend or portend to lead self-sufficient lives, nor must we claim to have a self-reliant heart. We must live like we need God and rely upon Him in everything. *Oh, Jesus, we ask for Your help in all that we think and do and say.* We must realize and admit that everything we have is a total gift from God and given to us on loan only—our money, our children, our ability to walk, our jobs, ad infinitum. We absolutely cannot operate and think for a minute that we do not need God. Our God is a god that takes great offense at such an attitude as would your spouse if you came home and said, *"You can live with me and take care of me, but I don't really need you."*

Those people who operate with the notion that they are totally self-reliant are in a trap that will surely cause them to sin and be displeasing to God. Many people depend only on themselves and thus claim to be self-reliant. This may seem right to us but its end is ultimately and surely death. In the last twenty years in this country especially, we have become so rich and have so many things our parents never had—cell phones, a computer in almost every house, a car at sixteen, pagers, etc. We travel all over, our kids participate in numerous sports, we belong to country clubs, we have summer homes, we have spending money—we have so much that many of us think we can take care of ourselves and that our money will get us whatever we want and need. We must never think that it is *stuff* that makes us happy. It is instead what we give away from our hearts that truly makes us happy.

My father, in his unending humility, taught us so much. He taught us never to take more from the earth than we needed, to give back to the earth whatever we didn't need, to always work hard, to help out whoever needed help without expecting repayment, and my very favorite, to remember that you *never* see a U-Haul behind a hearse. He taught us that money could not buy true happiness that lasted. It might pay to buy stuff but not true happiness. I think of my dad and what he taught us daily and, the older I get, the more I see how very wise he was. My father taught us total reliance on our God, and in his own simple and yet incredibly spiritual way, he taught us what it meant to be a servant of God.

We were never allowed to complain about what we had to eat in our house growing up because at least we had something to eat, my parents would say. We were never allowed to complain about having only one car because at least we had a car. We could never complain about our dad's meager income because at least he had a job. What valuable lessons these were. *"God, put us where we need to be,"* my parents would say, and "He puts before us opportunities to serve others through the people He has cross our lives." It was our duty to help whoever we could because we were given the ability to help them. There was never a question as to *whether* we would help someone in need—it was *always* a given and none of us ever questioned that. *Share your lunch with someone who doesn't have any; that's why you have more than you really need.* My mom always did laundry for someone other than our family, it seemed, whether for some widow she knew or a widower neighbor; she always made pies for our church festival; she always gave her homemade German Christmas cookies away to the neighbors and our teachers and those less fortunate. My parents made weekly visits to the nursing home, always taking along some little treat to make the residents there happy. They drove a couple to the grocery store each week because they didn't own a car. My dad delivered a $10 meat order to a lady each week because she didn't drive. They were true servants of God and we must be too.

The real tragedy of people today is that they hear the call of God, they know the will of God through His commandments, they receive the commands of God time and time again, and yet, they still are unwilling to follow God's command and do what God has called on them to do. In this century, especially, many people have decided to follow the "if it feels good, it's okay" philosophy or the "if I say it's okay, it's okay" philosophy or the "if I want to do it and it's not illegal, then it's okay" philosophy. They *follow the herd*, so to speak, and do things just because their neighbor is doing them or just because everybody else is doing them. They justify away following the commandments and if they do it often enough, they lose the guilt and shame they formerly felt when they broke God's laws. *I can take these supplies from the office because there are plenty of them and my boss won't miss them. I can lie to my mom about where I was last night because if I tell her the truth, she'll get mad at me. I can cheat on this test or I won't get into law school. I don't have to go to church on Sunday because no one else is going either. I can abort this baby because I can't afford it right now.* Pretty soon, there will not be too many things a person does that will invoke a feeling of guilt and shame anymore because, pretty much, anything goes.

The problem is that it doesn't matter what a person thinks or says to justify breaking or bending

God's commandments—in the end, that person will be held accountable for their actions in the eyes of God. God never said, "Follow My commandments if you *want* to," or "Follow My commandments if it's *convenient*," or "Follow My commandments *if you feel like it.*" His command was simple—*Follow My commandments*—PERIOD!

Many people feel too weak to stand up for what they know is right because they lack the confidence and courage they need. They do not think that God is with them because they have a self-reliant heart. There are so many pitfalls to a self-reliant heart. We must first and foremost trust in God in all that we do. Then we must obey God in all that He says. By doing these two things in that order, our lives will become so much more simple. The road to God is so straight and full of road signs. It is when we choose to make the journey without these road signs that the road becomes hazardous and full of curves. It is then that the road becomes full of chaos and that we get lost. It is then that we find ourselves afraid and alone and in trouble much of the time. We must move along our journey with honesty and integrity, forging the path for those who are to follow.

Even following God's commandments after learning to trust and obey God is not enough though.

We find many people who themselves have an awakening to die to themselves and become followers of Jesus Christ. But they do so kind of in hiding because they do not want to make waves, they do not want people to question them, they do not want people to make fun of them, they do not want people to ostracize them from their group, or they do not want to make people mad at them. Some would say that this type of person is very humble. But this is not true humility but fear. Remember, Joseph Stowell says, "The kingdom is not a field of wimps. We must be soldiers for Him." So we cannot just stand by and watch our friends and coworkers and family members continue justifying their lives and justifying twisting God's commandments to their convenience and breaking God's commandments because we do not want to make waves. We cannot just sit by and watch as others continue their journey without following God's road signs because it would be a little bit uncomfortable for us to say something. We cannot be soldiers for Him if we are too weak to fight for what we know is right. We cannot be His servants and servants to those around us if we are too timid to stand up for what we know is right. We must take responsibility.

It is so much easier to hide behind your excuses. *I can't preach to my teenager that I really want him to go to church on Sunday because he might not like me. I can't tell my coworker that it's wrong to have an abortion because I'm afraid she won't talk to be anymore. I can't tell my sister to forgive my brother for hurting her feelings last year because she'll tell me to mind my own business and start a fight with me.* Trusting God and obeying His command to go out to others and gently urging them to do the right thing is not easy—no one says it is. But once again, *the kingdom is not a field of wimps. We must be soldiers for Him.*

> *Dear good and gracious God!*
> *We once again stand before You weak*
> *   and broken, scared and alone.*
> *We ask for Your strength that we may learn to*
> *   listen to You, to become confident in Your*
> *   affirmations, to put our complete trust in*
> *   You, and to obey You without question.*
> *We ask that You free us from our self-reliance*
> *   and open our hearts to Yours.*
> *W we ask this all in the holy name of*
> *   Jesus Christ, Your Son, Amen.*

Gifts of the Holy Spirit

*Now to each one the manifestation of the
Spirit is given for the common good. To one, there
is given through the Spirit the message of wisdom,
to another the message of knowledge by means of
the same Spirit, to another faith by the same Spirit,
to another the gift of healing by that one Spirit, to
another miraculous powers, to another prophecy, to
another distinguishing between spirits, to another
speaking in different kinds of tongues, and to still
another the interpretation of tongues. All these
are the work of one and the same Spirit and He
gives them to each one, just as He determines.*
—Corinthians 12:7–11

L earn to become free in the knowledge of God's love. Free yourself to open your heart to the gifts of the Holy Spirit. Pray daily and pray unceasingly. And above all, pray with utmost confidence that our good and gracious God will listen to your prayers and answer them as He sees fit and when He sees fit. The Holy Spirit came down upon the apostles in their hiding and fear after Jesus Christ died. The apostles had just spent three years with Christ learning the ways of the kingdom of God, and then their beloved leader was taken from them and put to death. Now, they were alone and scared to death, for their leader was no longer there to tell them what to do and to lead them. It was in their hour of fear and prayer that God helped them know what they were to do next and that the Holy Spirit descended upon them and showered them with His gifts of wisdom and tongues. Suddenly, the apostles were filled with the Holy Spirit and literally transformed into true disciples of Christ, speaking in tongues so that all could understand and teaching in the name of Jesus Christ. From that day forward, they were no longer afraid and weak, but brave and strong. They were no longer uncertain and meek, but totally sure of themselves and outspoken in the truths of the kingdom of God. They evangelized whoever would listen and did so even in the midst of persecution and death. They had the affirmation of the Holy Spirit and were no longer afraid. They became soldiers of Jesus Christ from that day forward, and we also must do the same.

We too must pray for the gifts and the fruits of the Holy Spirit. Above all, we must pray for wisdom and humility, and once these are given to us, pretty much all of the other gifts and fruits will come for the asking. Those gifts and fruits are many and include understanding, knowledge, counsel, fortitude, piety, fear of the Lord, charity, joy, peace, patience, kindness, goodness, generosity, gentleness, faithfulness, modesty, self-control, chastity, mercy, forgiveness, hope, love, trust, discernment to make the right choices, fairness, compassion, courage to speak out against injustice and do something about it, clear vision, etc. With receiving the gifts and fruits of the Holy Spirit comes the obligation to use them, and not just to put them on a shelf somewhere. We must listen to God's call and His affirmations, and we must take action. When we see a street person, we must not cross the street but offer some sort of help—buy them a sandwich and a drink, give them a pair of shoes if they are barefoot, give them a coat if they are cold. If we see racial injustice, we must speak out against it. If our friends are drinking and getting ready to drive, we must take their keys away. If we are offered drugs, we must refuse them and speak out against drugs. If someone hurts our feelings, we must forgive them before the sun goes down and never bring it up again. We must change our world from one of *me, me, me* and do so with an unselfish and giving heart. We must show our quiet wisdom and unfaltering faith in all that we do, and we must become an inspiration to those whose paths we cross, shining through our gentle love on earth. We must strive to always have a compassionate and loving heart that will change the world around us a little bit each day with every small loving act that we do.

We must remember that being brave does not mean that we do not feel afraid—it merely means doing the right thing in spite of feeling afraid. "Therefore, gird the loins of your minds for action; keep sober in spirit, fix your hope completely on the grace to be brought to you at the revelation of Jesus Christ" (1 Peter 1:13). We must strive to say not just what the world wants to hear, but what we truly believe in and what is right. We must strive to do not just what the world thinks we should do, but what we know is right. We must strive to be not just what the world thinks we should be, but who we really are.

We must strive to listen without judgment, to value honesty over appearances, to value effort over accomplishments, to stand up for what is right, to give with true joy, to be humble in spirit, to rely on our good and gracious God for all that we think and do and say. We must serve the poorest of the poor, those who are struggling, those who are a little bit different, those who are not easy to love, those whose lives are not filled with dignity and respect, those who are down and out, those who are downtrodden, those who are sick, those who are hard on their luck, those who need us the most. We must be remembered and recognized as a slave of Jesus Christ, filled with the gifts of the Holy Spirit and always ready to share those gifts with all.

> *Dear good and gracious God!*
> *Help us to sort out all of our roles and*
> *make some sense of them.*
> *Help us to find the person You really want*
> *us to be and to be true to that self.*
> *Help us to realize that You never give*
> *us more than we can handle,*
> *And that these multiple demands on us are*
> *not meant to tear us apart but to add*
> *dimension to our lives—to make us whole.*

Help us to recognize and share the
gifts of Your spirit.
We ask this all in the holy name of Jesus
Christ, Your Son, Amen.

Peace

The spirit of the Lord God is upon me
Because the Lord has anointed me,
He has sent me to bring glad tidings to the lowly,
To heal the brokenhearted;
To proclaim liberty to the captive,
And release to the prisoners,
To announce a year of favor from the Lord,
And a day of vindication by our God,
To comfort all who mourn;
To place on those who mourn in Zion
a diadem instead of ashes;
To give them oil of gladness in place of mourning,
A glorious mantle instead of a listless spirit…
—Isaiah 61:1–3

Offer peace to all with whom you come in contact. Be of service to all. Judge not. Ask not why someone is in the condition or situation they are in—just offer them peace and help and unconditional love. Remember that it is not what a person may have done or not done that matters—it is what you do to help them and how you show your love for them that matters in the eyes of our God. Look at every day as a preparation for death. Realize that what the dying go through today, you will go through tomorrow. Try to live each day in the peace of Christ and offer your peace and love to those around you every day. Live each day as if it were your last so that you will always be ready and prepared to meet God and die with a clean heart. Love everyone without expectations. If you expect something in return and put conditions on your love, then it will not be true love. Show not your anger or fear or repulsion or disgust or judgment about those who cross your path. Simply serve them with love and offer them your peace in the name of the Lord so that their hearts and minds are filled with the peace of Jesus Christ. Let this peace radiate from you daily wherever you go and to whomever you meet. Remember always that you are not here to judge or chastise or belittle or be served. It is not your job to make a person feel bad about themselves or embarrassed to need your help or scared of how you may look at them. You must simply radiate God's love and peace and mercy at all times so that you can serve others as God would have you serve, and so that all around you may feel God's peace and love through you. Come in the peace of God and go in the peace of God. Seek not to judge or to ask why or how. Simply offer God's peace to all.

> *Lord, make me an instrument of Thy peace!*
> *Where there is hatred, let me sow love.*
> *Where is injury, pardon.*
> *Where there is discord, harmony.*
> *Where there is doubt, faith.*
> *Where is despair, hope.*
> *Where there is darkness, light.*
> *Where there is sorrow, joy.*
> *Oh, Divine Master, grant that I may not so*
> *much seek to be consoled as to console;*
> *To be understood as to understand;*
> *To be loved as to love.*
> *For it is in giving that we receive,*
> *It is in pardoning that we are pardoned,*
> *And it is in dying that we are born to eternal*
> *life* (Prayer of St. Francis of Assisi).

Dear good and gracious God!
Help us to sort out all of our roles and
make some sense of them.
Help us to find the person You really want
us to be and to be true to that self.
Help us to realize that You never give
us more than we can handle.
Help us to realize that the multiple challenges
given to us are not meant to tear us apart,
But are given to us to add dimension to
our lives and to make us whole.
We ask this all through the most holy name
of Jesus Christ, Your Son, Amen.

Faith

*What doth it profit a man if he
has faith and not works?*
—James 2:14

Without faith in our God, we cannot serve others. Mother Teresa walked a simple path that consisted of silence to hear the word of God, unceasing prayer, and deep faith that God would provide the gifts needed to do His will, love of all, service to the poorest of the poor, and peace to all. She said, "Be faithful in small things because is in them that your strength lies."

To Mother Teresa, every work of love done with a loving heart always brings a person closer to their God. It is in the silence of the heart that God speaks. We cannot hear God if we are not completely silent and open to His word and if we are not completely faithful to His teachings. We must completely empty ourselves and be completely still and open to His word so that God can speak to us and so that we can hear what He has to say. Mother Teresa said, "I do not pray for success; I ask for faithfulness."

Have faith and total trust in God that He hears your prayers and will give you guidance in what you are to do. Have faith in God that He will put you where He wants you when He wants you there, and that He will give you what you need. Trust that you will meet the people He wants you to meet and will walk with you. Have faith in Him and take whatever He gives you with a big smile. To those of you that He gives much wealth, you should make use of it wisely and try to share it with others, especially with those who have nothing. You should always share with those less fortunate because, many times, even with a little help, you may be able to save a person from great distress or even despair with only a little. To give to those who do not need it is not doing God's work for they do not need the gift. To give to those in despair and in great need fills a void and can change despair into hope. And if you are blessed with great wealth, never take more than you need. Keep life simple and remember that *you never see a U-Haul behind a hearse.*

"Don't be discouraged at those times when you question, when you doubt, when you don't understand. There is a darkness in faith. There is that uncertainty, an insecurity in trusting God. Yet, He demands that we believe without seeing, we don't know why things are happening and we certainly don't know what's going to happen. But you must know that the darkness you experience and the anxiety you experience are not a lack of trust; they're part of trust. You've got to let yourself go and persevere in faith" (Arroyo 2007).

Have the faith to see God in everyone and love your neighbor as yourself. See all life as precious and do not judge. Realize that it is not for humans to decide who will live and who will die, and realize that an unborn baby is no more guilty and deserving of being put to death as is a child in a refugee camp that is already born. Have the faith to serve all who come onto your path that need help, be it to serve those who simply need a smile, a coat, a job, a meal, a friend, a ride to the doctor, etc. Make a difference and do something for those less fortunate than you—the widow, the sick, the lonely, the frightened, the hungry, the homeless, the ugly, the unwanted, the outcasts of society. Have faith that you can make a difference in the life of one person at a time. Volunteer in a soup kitchen, visit a shut-in, drive someone to the doctor's office, go to the grocery store for a shut-in, help someone in need. All life is precious—try to improve the lives of all those with whom you come into contact. Have the faith to become like a pebble that is thrown into the sea that causes a ripple effect. A ripple can be made by one small act of service that can become the start of many. Strive to be the person that starts the ripple effect.

"More than ever I find myself in the hands of God. This is what I have wanted all my life from my youth. But now there is a difference; the initiative is entirely with God. It is indeed a profound spiritual experience to know and feel myself so totally in God's hands" (Fr. Pedro Arrupe, who composed this reflection following his stroke).

Trust God and reach out to serve others in faith—to help your fellow man, to be there when they are in need. Do not wait for them to ask for your help for some people simply cannot or will not ask for your help. Seek out the needs of others and do not be afraid to help them in any way you can. Remember that every small act of kindness will be noticed and will not be forgotten either by those you help or by God. Remember that "Not everyone that saith unto me, 'Lord, Lord' shall enter into the kingdom of heaven, but he that doeth the will of my Father who is in heaven. Many will say to me in that day, 'Lord, Lord, have we not prophesied in Thy name, and in Thy name have cast out devils, and in Thy name done many wonderful works?' And then will I profess unto them, 'I never knew you; depart from me, ye that work iniquity'" (Matt. 7:27–28).

Dear good and gracious God!
Strengthen our faith, Lord.
When we fall, help us up.
When we become weak, enlighten us.
When we feel despair, give us hope.
When we are tired, renew our energy,
So that we can help others in the journey of faith,
And enable all to become the better
    person they can become.
We ask this all in the most holy name of
    Jesus Christ, Your Son, Amen.

Rules to Enable
Us to Serve

He said to them,
"Is a lamp brought in to be placed under
a bushel basket or under a bed,
And not to be placed on a lamp stand?
For there is nothing hidden except
to be made visible…"
—Mark 4:21–25

S erving others need not have its own set of rules,
but there are those that may be hesitant or unable
to serve without them. So, here are some good rules

to learn and hearken to in our quest to spend our lives in service to others:

- *"Knowledge without action—it is called sickness"* (Zhuang Zi).
- *"The heavier the responsibility, the greater the virtue, the better the effects, the higher the level"* (Xun Zi).
- *"Sages do not display themselves; therefore, they are illuminated. They do not define themselves; therefore, they are distinguished. They do not make claims; therefore, they are credited. They do not boast; therefore, they advance"* (Dao De Jing, Tao of Power, Passage 22).
- *"Therefore, to rise above people, one must, in speaking, stay below them. To remain in front of people, one must be one step behind them"* (Dao De Jing, Tao of Power, Passage 66).
- *"If I have helped others, I should not think about it. If I have wronged others, I should think about it. If others have helped me, I should not forget about it. If others have wronged me, I should forget about it"* (Zen).

- *"Instead of planning for something you cannot do, concentrate on the strengths that you already have. Instead of regretting past mistakes, work to prevent future errors"* (Zen).

- *"Daily I examine my person on three counts—in my undertakings on behalf of other people—have I failed to do my utmost? In my interactions with colleagues and friends—have I failed to make good to my word? In what is passed onto me—have I failed to carry it into practice?"* (Master Zeng).

- *"In strolling in the company of just two other persons, I am bound to find a teacher. Identifying their strengths, I follow them, and identifying their weaknesses, I reform myself accordingly"* (Confucius).

- *"God cannot be realized if there is the slightest attachment to the things of the world"* (Ramakrishna).

- *"Most misery and inability on earth is caused by man and woman having forgotten how to love one another. But it means doing day by day that which is known, that which is proven, that which is expressed today in keeping with what He would have thee do. Thus, ye find that ye do first things first; that is, the thought of self not so much as self-pres-ervation from want, care, discouragement, and the like, but rather as to just be gentle, just being kind. For righteousness, which is taking time to be righteous, is just speaking gently, even when harsh words, harsh means are resorted to by others. This is what is meant by 'turn the other cheek;' and know the Lord standeth with thee"* ("Spiritual Breakthrough," Todechi, A.R.E.).

- *"According to a great wisdom tradition of India, there are three worldly ways to become intricate with divine intelligence or God:*
  - *Selfless service, doing good to others with-out a desire for personal gain* (Seva);
  - *Remembrance in God, remembrance of our purpose in life, and remem-brance through prayer and meditation* (Simrau) *and,*
  - *Through a gathering of people seeking the truth"* (Satsang).
- *"Remember that you become what you focus on. Focus on being God's servant and you cannot help but become God's servant The ultimate aim in life of every human soul should be to attain moral and spiritual excel-*

lence, not to align one's inner being and out-
ward behavior with the will of an all-loving
Creator" (Bahá'u'lláh).

- *"Be general in prosperity, and thankful in*
adversity. Be worthy of the trust of thy neigh-
bor, and look upon him with a bright and
friendly face. Be a treasure to the poor, an
admonisher to the rich, an answerer of the cry
of the needy, a preserver of the sanctity of thy
pledge. Be fair in thy judgment, and guarded
in thy speech. Be unjust to no man, and show
all meekness to all men" (Bahá'u'lláh).
- *"Be as a lamp unto them that walk in dark-*
ness" (Bahá'u'lláh).
- *"Take into account that great love and great*
achievements involve great risks" (Dalai Lama).
- *"When you lose, do not lose the lesson"* (Dalai
Lama).
- *"Follow the three R's: Respect for self; respect*
for others; and responsibility for all of your
actions" (Dalai Lama).
- *"When you realize you have made a mistake,*
take immediate steps to correct it" (Dalai
Lama).

- *"Spend some time alone in the classroom of silence every day to listen for the word of God"* (Matthew Kelly).
- *"Open your arms to change, but do not let go of your values"* (Dalai Lama).
- *"A loving atmosphere in your home is the foundation for your life"* (Mother Teresa).
- *"Live a good and honorable life; then when you look back, you'll be able to enjoy it a second time"* (Dalai Lama).
- *"See the distressing face of Christ in everyone you meet"* (Mother Teresa).

Dear good and gracious God!
Teach me Your rules.
Teach me to see.
Teach me to listen.
Teach me to hear.
Teach me to be Your true and faithful
*   servant unto death.*
We ask this all in the most holy name of
*   Jesus Christ, Your Son, Amen.*

How to Love God and Become Spiritually Successful

You shall love the Lord, your God,
with all your heart,
With all your being,
With all your strength,
And with all your mind,
And your neighbor as yourself.
—Luke 10:27–28

T here are so many ways to love God, but we must strive daily to recommit ourselves in these ways and must live our lives reflecting these ways. To love God, we must love our fellow human beings and all of them—not just our friends, not just those of our religion, not just those of our race, not just those with our political beliefs, not just those with our education level, not just those with our socioeconomic status. We must love *all* of our fellow human beings—of all religious beliefs, of all races, of all political views, of all educational levels or lack thereof, of all socio-economic levels, etc. We must love those who love us and those who hate us, those who irritate us and those who please us, those we find pretty and those we find ugly, those we can tolerate and those we cannot, those who are good to us and those who are not, those who are there for us and those who are not, those who praise us and those who bring us down, those who like us and those who ridicule us.

"If we endure our trials and tribulations with patience and contentment, accepting this as God's will, we are loving God. If, instead of seeing faults in others, we look within ourselves, we are loving God. If, instead of robbing others to help ourselves, we rob ourselves to help others, we are loving God. If we suffer in the sufferings of others and feel happy in the happiness of others, we are loving God. If, instead of worrying over our own misfortunes, we think of ourselves as more fortunate than many and don't complain, we are loving God. If we understand and feel that the greatest act of devotion and worship of our God is not to hurt any of His beings, we are loving God" (Meher Baba).

In order to attain spiritual success and be able to act as a servant of God to others, we must constantly evaluate the consequences of our choices—will our choice bring happiness or assurance to those in need? We must remember that "a man's true wealth is the good he does in this world" (Muhammed). We must listen with our hearts to hear the will of God. Continually ask God for guidance and allow yourself to be guided by His spirit.

We must take ownership and responsibility for our own actions and not blame others for our actions. We must practice acceptance of others. We must not judge others. Practice nonjudgment. Say to yourself, "Today I will not judge anything or anyone." We must show unconditional love to others. We should give something to everyone we meet. This does not have to be something of monetary value. It can be a smile, a compliment, a helping hand, a listening ear, a moment of our time. We must be open to receive from others so that our needs to receive can also be met. We should make the commitment to be available at all times and open to the needs of others. If we limit our availability, we might miss valuable opportunities to serve. We should open ourselves to limitless opportunities to serve others. We should look to help everyone with whom we come into contact in some small way. We should continually ask ourselves how we can help others. Rather than trying to find what's in it for you, share more and treat people like your brothers and sisters in Christ.

> *Dear good and gracious God!*
> *Teach me how to pray, Lord.*
> *Teach me how to hear you, Lord.*
> *Teach me how to listen to You, Lord.*
> *Teach me how to see Your face in all I meet, Lord.*
> *Teach me not to be afraid, Lord.*
> *Teach me that I am no better than*
>   *anyone else, Lord.*
> *Teach me that I am Your servant, Lord.*
> *We ask this all in the most holy name of*
>   *Jesus Christ, Your Son, Amen.*

Listening

Whoever exalts himself will be humbled,
But whoever humbles himself will be exalted.
—Matthew 23:12

" Listening is knowing what, when, and how something is being said. Listening is distinguishing what is not being said from what is silence. Listening is not acting like you are in a hurry, even if you are. Listening is eye contact, a hand placed gently upon an arm. Sometimes, listening is taking careful notes in the person's own words. Listening involves suspension of judgment" (Allison Para Bastien). Never be afraid to listen to a person's story, to their heart, to their fears, to their anxieties, to their questions, to their concerns. For it is in listening that we come to understand, it is in listening that we come to hear, it is in listening that we are illuminated, it is in listening that we show our love and concern, it is in listening that we allow a person to share their life. We serve when we listen and not judge, when we listen and not give advice, when we just listen.

Mother Teresa tells us: "Before you speak, it is necessary for you to listen, for God speaks in the silence of the heart." It is in silence that we hear; it is in not giving advice unless we are asked for it that we listen; it is when we are not obsessed with ourselves, that we can listen; it is when we are truly detached from time that we can listen; it is when we are generous with our time that we can listen; it is when we allow someone to show us exactly what is on their mind that we really listen; and it is when we allow a person to really be themselves when they speak that we really listen. Listen and hear; listen and love; listen and be silent—this is truly listening. Listen kindly and tenderly to them. Let your face show kindness and understanding and acceptance and nonjudgment and warmth. Listen not only with your ears but with your heart.

Dear good and gracious God!
Teach me to be still.
Teach me to have time.
Teach me to not judge.
Teach me to not preach.
Teach me the beauty of silence.
Teach me to hear through Your ears.
We ask this all in the most holy name of
     Jesus Christ, Your Son, Amen.

Humility

Humble yourselves therefore under
the mighty hand of God,
That He may exalt you in due time.
—1 Peter: 5–6

H*umility* is defined as "being low in station, unimportant, lowly." The Spirit of Christ is aware of only one thing and that is a perfect union with the Father. In Matthew 11:29, Jesus says, "Take My yoke upon you and learn from Me, for I am gentle and humble in heart, and you will find rest for your souls." Everything we do should be achieved in perfect union *with* our God and *for* our God instead of based on a self-willed determination to be holy. We must do whatever we do not in the spirit of self-satisfaction, but in the meek and quiet spirit of our God. "I do not count on my merits because I have none but God" (St. Therese of Liseiux).

"Humility is perfect quietness of heart. It is to have no trouble. It is never to be fretted or irritated or sore or disappointed. It is to expect nothing, to wonder at nothing that is done to me. It is to be at rest when nobody praises me and when I am blamed or despised. It is to have a blessed home in the Lord, where I can go in and shut the door and kneel to my Father in secret, and I am at peace as in the deep sea of calmness when all around and above have trouble" (author unknown). One cannot fully love others if they do not first die to themselves. We must first go on our own journey in order to come to a personal realization of where we are in our own spiritual awakening, in our own spiritual journey. Though this journey may take us through sadness and guilt and fear and difficulties and areas of suffering and doubts, it is through the awakening that we express on this journey and through these self-awarenesses who we are and where we are going that we learn the humility necessary to recognize our limitations, our imperfections, and our need for God. It is here that we discover our inner strength and dependence on our God and His total and unconditional love for us. It is through these discoveries that we are able to escape and emerge from and surrender our old habits and weaknesses and gain our freedom to follow our spiritual paths. "When little obstacles crop up on the spiritual path, a good practitioner does not lose faith and begin to doubt, but has the discernment to recognize difficulties, whatever they may be, for what they are—just obstacles, and nothing more" (Sogyal Rinpoche). We must do everything that we can to the best of our ability in this life, and we must choose to do it all for the greater glory of our God and according to His plan.

William Carey ordered the following verse to be placed on his tomb:

> *A guilty, weak, and helpless worm.*
> *On Christ's kind arms I fall.*
> *He is my strength, my righteousness,*
> *My Jesus and my all.*

Remember that the major value in life is not what you get but what you become. Instead of being concerned about what you do not have and feeling sorry for yourself, one should make it a practice to look down the socio-economic ladder instead of up.

That way, it puts things into perspective and shows us just how grateful we should be and how much we really have. "It is when we as God's congregation of saplings, so to speak, grow from mere saplings to a fortified wood, and when we live with enough humility to wash the feet of others, that we bring new life and light to those whose hearts were previously hidden beneath bushel baskets" (Reynolds, *The Criterion*, 07-28-06). "We must never glance at what is good in ourselves, much less ponder of it, but we should search out what is wrong and what is lacking. This is an excellent way of remaining humble" (St. Vincent DePaul, 1580–1660). As Jonathan Edwards once wrote, "Nothing sets a person so much out of the devil's reach as humility."

We should also remember that everything we have has been given to us. Even though we work hard for what we have, it is God who chose us for some unknown reason to have the opportunities we have to get what we have. Think for a moment why you were born where you were instead of in India, or why you are able to work and someone else is not. Although we will never know the answers to these questions in this lifetime, we should be grateful for God's many blessings upon us, and be ever grateful for all that we have. "As great the work that God may achieve by an individual, he must not indulge in self-satisfaction. He ought rather to be all the more humbled, seeing himself merely as a tool which God has made of him" (St. Vincent DePaul, 1580–1660). "Most of us die with symphonies unfinished. While we are on earth, we are to play the melody" (author unknown).

> *Dear good and gracious God!*
> *Teach me today to be thankful for what I have.*
> *To not complain about what I do not have.*
> *To not think I deserve more.*
> *And to not feel sorry for myself.*
> *Instead, Lord, teach me to sing Your praises,*
> *And to be ever grateful for my abilities*
> *   and for my many blessings.*
> *We ask this all in the most holy name of*
> *   Jesus Christ, Your Son, Amen.*

Hearing the Call of God

"But this is the covenant that I will make
with the house of Israel after those days," says the Lord:
"I will put My law within them,
And I will write it upon their hearts;
And I will be their God,
And they shall be My people."
—Jeremiah 31:33

O ur God speaks to us through the scriptures and through the prophets. He tells us in many ways to listen to Him and to hear His word, to listen to Him and to follow His commands, to listen to Him and to seek His approval, to listen to Him, and to walk with Him on His journey. He gives us many road signs along the way and talks to us of a narrow gate through which we must pass to gain entrance into His kingdom. He talks to us about fishing to find each one of us: "Come after Me and I will make you fishers of men" (Mark 1:17). The call of our God cannot be heard if we listen for a call that is the reflection of our own desires, our own personal temperament, our own affinities, our own likes and dislikes. When we are brought into a true relationship with God, we must totally and completely be able to say, *let go, let God.* We must listen not for a call that suits us or answers our pleas. We can only hear the call of God if our lives have been profoundly altered, and we are open and willing to listen with our hearts. God gathers us into a relationship with Him so that we do things for others out of sheer love for Him. Service is the overflow of superabounding devotion and love for our God. Service to others will become a natural part of our lives when we hear the call of God. Service to others is our expression of God's love for us that we pass onto others. We must first be completely still and *enter into the classroom of silence* as Matthew Kelly calls it. In this classroom of silence, we must be completely quiet and empty ourselves of everything else in our life until we are totally quiet. It is in this total silence and quiet that we must listen and try to hear the voice of our God speaking to us. We must remember that, as workers for God, we must make room for God. We must always be in a state of expectancy and leave room for God to enter in whenever He likes. Get into the habit of saying to God, "Speak, Lord, I am listening." Say this every time you feel uncertain and then make time to listen. Be constantly opening your ears to hear the call of God.

Doing good works are visible signs that express our faith to others. These good works cause us to be a light that shines for the world to see—a sign of Christ's presence among us. "If I am not doing the works of my Father, then do not believe me; but if I do them, even though you do not believe me, believe the works, that you may know and understand that the Father is in me and I am in the Father" (John 10:37–38).

The needs of our fellow human beings are as great as ever. It is in the treatment of each other that our true greatness shines through. Ask yourself each day, each minute, what it is that you can do to make a positive difference in the life of someone else. Could you give a smile to a stranger, comfort to a child, help to an elderly neighbor? Could you give of your time and talents to a special cause dear to your heart? If so, get up now and give of yourself unconditionally, and in so doing, you will be helping yourself and your spiritual development.

> *Dear good and gracious God!*
> *Let us listen today so that we can hear Your call,*
> *Let us open our hearts so that we do*
> *not ignore the cry of the poor,*
> *Let us hear through Your ears so that*
> *we recognize those in need,*
> *And realize how we can answer their call for*
> *help and understanding and love.*
> *We ask this all in the most holy name of*
> *Jesus Christ, Your Son, Amen.*

Forgiveness

Then Peter came to Jesus and asked,
"Lord, how many times shall I forgive my
brother when he sins against me?
Up to seven times?"
Jesus answered, "I tell you,
Not seven times, but seventy-seven times seven."
—Matthew 18:21–22

You may think that you can be a true servant of God and serve others no matter what, but if you harbor anger, hatred, past hurts, or bad feelings against anyone in your life, you cannot truly act as God's servant. For God said, *"And when you stand praying, if you hold anything against anyone, forgive him, so that your Father in heaven may forgive you your sins"* (Mark 11:25). *"Do not judge, and you will not be judged. Do not condemn, and you will not be condemned. Forgive, and you will be forgiven"* (Luke 6:37). God did not make forgiveness of others an option. He made it a demand. You may think it is impossible to forgive someone who has deeply hurt you, but with God, it is possible for He never asks us to do anything we cannot do, and He is always there to help us do it, no matter how difficult. God made it clear throughout the Bible that those who forgive others reap the greatest benefits from forgiving—not those who are forgiven. The process of forgiving others releases us from anger and resentment, and allows us to receive God's healing. The spirit of unforgiveness hinders and compromises our walk with our God and puts a barrier between us and Him. God does not make exceptions to forgiveness or put certain sins to forgive ahead of others. He tells us to forgive everyone and to do it immediately before coming to His altar to pray. We must remember that forgiving hurts or past offenses does not justify or condone the sin of the person, nor does it provide God's forgiveness for their actions, for only God can do that. But God is very clear on His command that we must forgive—

PERIOD! "If we forgive others their transgressions, God will also forgive us; but if we do not forgive others, then God will not forgive your transgressions" (Matt. 6:14).

Forgiveness means letting go or putting away—letting go of the anger, the hurt, the resentment, the past problems. It means loving your enemies as God commands. We must learn how to forgive. It is not easy, it sometimes takes a long time, and it is sometimes not possible without God's help. Forgiveness is not a feeling or an emotion—it is instead a conscious decision on our part to stop holding on to past offenses against another. When we truly forgive someone, we must totally release them and forget it. While nothing can be done to change what has taken place or undo it, forgiving others allows our own healing to begin. Forgiving others must start as a decision on our part and an invitation to God to begin working in our lives and enlightening us with the understanding that we need to forgive with our hearts. If we really want to love, we must first learn how to forgive. "Forgiveness is the fragrance the violet sheds on the heel that has crushed it" (Mark Twain).

Sometimes before we can truly forgive others, we must first learn to forgive ourselves and feel that we are worthy in God's eyes to be forgiven for some of our own past sins. Before we can do that, we must first acknowledge that we have sinned and that we need forgiveness. That is why denial and justification for something in our past that we know is wrong are so devastating. Pretending something did not happen or trying to justify that it was ok makes us vulnerable and keeps us in a state of not feeling like we need forgiveness. Or, even worse, it may keep us in a state where we feel unworthy to even presume that our sins can be forgiven and leaves us in a sort of abyss from which we feel we cannot escape. "When I kept silent about my sins, my body wasted away through my groaning all day long. For day and night, Thy hand was heavy upon me; my moisture is turned into the drought of summer. I acknowledged my sin unto Thee, and my sins I have not hid. I said, 'I will confess my transgressions unto the Lord;' and Thou forgave the guilt of my sin" (Psalm 32:3–5). If we want to experience God's forgiveness, we must wholeheartedly admit that we have done wrong, ask for God's forgiveness, and be truly sorry for the offense. And then we will be freed in the knowledge that our loving and merciful God forgives us. "As far as the east is from the west, so far has He removed our transgressions from us" (Psalm 103:12). We must never think that our sins are so appalling that they are unforgivable and that God cannot forgive them. And we must know that every time we admit our wrongs and ask for God's forgiveness, God will grant us forgiveness. He loves us unconditionally and will forgive us whenever we sincerely ask Him to for He is a God of mercy and compassion and unconditional love.

We often think of forgiveness as something that someone who has done us harm or wrong must ask of us. But instead, God asks us to place our focus on offering forgiveness to the person who has wronged us. To not forgive someone is like taking the poison (continuing to suffer for what they did or did not do to you) and expecting *them* to die!

The greatest fallacy about forgiveness is the thought that forgiving the offense or wrongdoing of another means that one condones it. This is far from the truth. In fact, one can only forgive what one knows to be wrong. Forgiveness does not mean that a person must reconcile with a person who has treated them badly or hurt them. Another misconception is the idea that forgiveness must depend upon whether or not the person who did you wrong apologizes or vows to change their ways. If this were the case and a wrongdoer's poor behavior were the primary determinant for a person's healing, then the wrongdoer in your life would retain control and power over you. Forgiveness instead is the expression of a person finding an inner peace and tranquility that can neither be stopped nor compelled by another. Many times, withholding forgiveness is a choice that makes a victim continue to remain the victim. We must remember that hurts will not heal until they are forgiven. Reliving hurts and injuries do nothing more than re-open wounds. So we should focus our energy on healing instead of the hurt through forgiveness. Remember, the person who has been hurt has two alternatives—to be destroyed by resentment, which leads to death; or to forgive, which leads to healing and life.

There is lots of dishonesty out there that sometimes tricks a person into thinking that once they have been saved and granted salvation, they no longer have to worry about anything—about their future sins, about whether or not they forgive others, about how they live their lives. This is not what Jesus taught. Instead, Jesus taught that a person who has been saved by faith in Him must forgive others always, or their future sins committed after their salvation will not be forgiven. We must not be tricked into thinking that *once we are saved, we will always be saved, no matter what.* In the Bible, God is very clear to explain very thoroughly that this is not true. He reminds us first of all that everyone, no matter what, is sinned against by others—many times by family and friends and those one holds most dear. He also reminds us that no matter how badly we are sinned against by others, we offend God much more severely and intensely by our sins against Him than anyone else does when they sin against us. And more than anything, he reminds us that he who treats his fellow man with any less mercy and love and forgiveness than our heavenly Father treats us for our sins will be punished and treated in the same way that the *wicked servant* referred to in Matthew's gospel treated his fellow man. "This is why the kingdom of heaven may be likened to a king who decided to settle accounts with his servants. When he began the accounting, a debtor was brought before him who owed him a huge amount. Since he had no way of paying it back, his master ordered him to be sold, along with his wife, his children, and all his property, in payment of the debt. At that, the servant fell down, did him homage, and said, 'Be patient with me, and I will pay you back in full.' Moved with compassion, the master of that servant let him go and forgave him the loan. When that servant had left, he found one of his fellow servants who owed him a much smaller amount. He seized him and started to choke him, demanding,

'Pay back what you owe.' Falling to his knees, his fellow servant begged him, 'Be patient with me, and I will pay you back.' But he refused and instead had him put in prison until he paid back the debt. Now, when his fellow servants saw what had happened, they were deeply disturbed, and went to their master and reported the whole affair. His master summoned him and said to him, 'You wicked servant! I forgave you your entire debt because you begged me to. Should you not have had pity on your fellow servant, as I had pity on you?' Then in anger, his master handed him over to the torturers until he should pay back the whole debt. So will my heavenly Father do to you unless each of you forgives his brother from his heart" (Matt. 18:21–35). Remember that there is a difference between *lip* forgiveness and *heart* forgiveness. Jesus cautioned us that we can expect pardon from our God only when we are willing to extend forgiveness to others *from your heart* (Matt. 18:35).

God tells us in scripture not to harbor anger and bitterness or a feeling of revenge against those who have hurt us or sinned against us. We must let those things go, He tells us, and let judgment and vengeance be His. "Do not take revenge, my friends, but leave room for God's wrath, for it is written: 'It is mine to avenge; I will repay,' says the Lord" (Rom.

12:19). There are many references in scripture to what God's expectations for us are in the arena of forgiveness: "The forgiving person is not merely passive in waiting for the offender to repent; he actively seeks the repentance of the one who wronged him" (Matt. 18:15–17); "The forgiving person is kindly disposed and tenderhearted toward his adversary" (Eph. 4:32); "The forgiving person does not attempt to take revenge upon those who have wronged him" (Rom. 12:17); and, "It is a rather terrible thing when we forget the many sins of which we've been forgiven" (2 Peter 1:9).

We must be honest with ourselves and consciously and openly reflect upon our own past and become openly (and painfully) aware of how often we too have disappointed the Lord so very terribly. Human nature makes us minimize our own mistakes yet maximize those of others. But we are "to speak evil of no one, not to be contentious, to be gentle, showing all humility toward all men. For we were also once foolish, disobedient, deceived, serving various lusts and pleasures, living in malice and envy, hateful, and hating one another. But when the kindness of God our Savior and His love toward mankind appeared, not by works of righteousness, which we did ourselves, but according to His mercy, He saved us, through the washing of regeneration and renewing by the Holy Spirit, which He poured out on us richly, through Jesus Christ our Savior; that, being justified by His grace, we might be made heirs according to the hope of eternal life" (Titus 3:2–7).

We should look at forgiveness as a gift to ourselves and not something we do for another; for our refusal to forgive by holding onto the anger or resentment toward another can make our lives miserable and does not usually hurt the other person at all. It is through forgiveness that we are changed from being prisoners of the past to free people. It is not forgetting but does involve accepting the promise that past injuries can be forgotten. If you are at war with others, you cannot be at peace with yourself. Living with resentment creates an incredible void in and around us and allows feelings of resentment and anger and hatred to seep into all areas of our lives, turning us into bitter, angry, unhappy, and frustrated individuals. Remember that no one benefits more from forgiveness than the one who forgives.

Dear good and gracious God!
You have loved me from the
moment of my creation,

You've forgiven me for the things I
thought were unforgiveable.
You've stood by me during the times
when nobody wanted to.
You've shown me miraculous and beautiful
things I thought were impossible.
You've taught me things a lifetime of
experience could never teach.
You've given me the gifts of life, love,
wisdom and happiness.
Now that You have done all this, I can
return your favor by loving, forgiving,
standing by, showing, teaching, and
given to your people as You did for me.
God, help me to have peace of mind and
a sense of moral confidence
To know in my heart what is right and wrong.
Give me strength to make wise decisions and
the courage to stand by my convictions—
Even in the face of adversity or
pressure from my peers.
Help me to be happy with myself and
the path I have taken.
And love me when I stray from what is right,
so that Your love may be my guide.

Let me practice forgiveness today by
    starting with the little hurts.
Let me realize today all the little things
    that do not go my way,
And call upon Your loving and peaceful presence,
And Your divine grace to surround me.
Let me pray today to consciously make the
    decision to unburden and detach myself
From the painful memories of the past,
And release to You all that slows me
    on my spiritual journey.
Give me the strength and courage today to begin
    to let go and forgive and release the past.
We ask this all in the most holy name of
    Jesus Christ, Your Son, Amen.

Learning to Become God's Servant

And God spoke to Israel in a vision at night and said,
"Jacob! Jacob!"
"Here I am, Lord," he replied.
—Genesis 46:2

G od calls on all of us to not only follow Him,
but also to do His will. While this may sound
easy, it is probably one of the most difficult things
in the world to do, for to truly follow Him and do
His will, we must die to self and put God first. And
we must be willing to take the road less traveled, the
lonelier road, the curvier road, the road with more

roadblocks. We must be willing to stand up to adversity, to ridicule, to derision, to scorn, to laughter, to mockery. We must be friends to those who have no friends, to those whom others avoid, to those most people may not like, to those that are outcasts, to those who have nothing. We must be willing to give to those less fortunate, to those who have nothing to give in return, to those who may not appreciate what we do. We must be willing to stand up for what is right and speak up against what is wrong, no matter how lonely a job that may be. We must put our faith and trust in our God that He will always give us the grace to do the jobs he puts in front of us to do, and not be afraid to answer Him when he calls by saying, *"Here I am, Lord, I come to do Your will."* That is what it is to be a servant of God. We are told over and over in Scripture that the place of a servant in God's eyes was a place of honor, a place of esteem, a place one could be proud to be. It is the only position in life where one can feel confident that God wants us to be for it is the position that Jesus Christ Himself took during His life on this earth. It is not a position of lowliness or shame, but one that is held in the highest regard by our God. It is a position we all should strive to find ourselves in, no matter what, and a position we should be proud of and hold our heads high in.

"Be holy. Therefore, prepare your minds for action; be self-controlled; set your hope fully on the grace to be given you when Jesus Christ is revealed" (Peter 1:13).

Love is everything. Jesus loved us so much that He suffered and died on the cross to save us. It only follows that we too should walk in love. "Since God chose you to be the holy people whom He loves, you must clothe yourselves with tenderhearted mercy.... You must make allowance for each other's faults and forgive the person who offends you. Remember, the Lord forgave you so you must forgive others. And the most important piece of clothing you must wear is love. Love is what binds us all together in perfect harmony" (Col. 3:12–14). Many times, God's children fail to realize the great value and absolute necessity of loving and serving each other, and that their very purpose on this earth is to love and to serve others. This comes from a lack of faith and belief in the overwhelming and total love of our God for us. It is when we gain insight into how deep and complete God's love is for us that this love spills over from us to others, and enables and empowers us to be servants to others. God tells us, "If I, your Master, have washed your feet, so you must wash the feet of others" (John 13:14).

Love for others results in serving others. It is in giving that we receive, and through good works to others that we do the will of our Father. As little or as much as we have, we can always look around and see greater needs than our own. It is our responsibility to recognize those needs and to do something about them. The ways we should serve are placed in front of us in many ways, and opportunities to serve are everywhere. First, we should serve those with whom we live, for love should start at home. Then, our love must radiate out from there in all that we do. The opportunities to serve are endless, and sometimes only a split second may be given to us to seize those opportunities. Let someone in front of you in traffic, pick up something someone has dropped, drive a shut-in to the doctor, give a sandwich to a homeless person, smile at someone who is obviously hurting, put your arm around someone who needs a hug, sit with a family member whose loved one is dying, pray for the dead, bring flowers to the sick, cook a meal for someone who is alone, babysit for a new mom—the list can go on and on. Do not miss the opportunities to radiate Christ's love to those around you. *"Follow God's example in everything you do, because you are His dear children. Live a life filled with love for others, following the example of Christ, who loved you*

and gave Himself as a sacrifice to take away your sins"
(Eph. 5:1–2).

> *Dear good and gracious God!*
> *Teach us the humility we need to be Your servant*
> *Give us the strength we need to do Your will,*
> *And the knowledge we need to know Your will.*
> *Give us the courage we need to stay strong*
>   *and not falter under fire,*
> *And the grace we need to carry out that which*
>   *You put us on this earth to accomplish.*
> *We ask this all in the most holy name of*
>   *Jesus Christ, Your Son, Amen.*

The Misconceptions
of Thinking You Can
Do It on Your Own

I asked God for strength, that I might achieve,
I was made weak, that I might learn humbly to obey;
I asked for health, that I might do greater things,
I was given infirmity, that I might do better things;
I asked for riches, that I might be happy,
I was given poverty, that I might be wise;
I asked for power, that I might have the praise of man,
I was given weakness, that I might feel the need of God;
I asked for all things, that I might enjoy life,
I was given life, that I might enjoy things;
I got nothing that I asked for—but
everything I had hoped for,

Almost despite myself, my unspoken
prayers were answered,
I am among all men, most richly blessed.
—Author Unknown

I t is sometimes easy for people who are very successful financially to get the feeling that they have
made it on their own and can do things on their own
without any help from anyone. Because, you know,
money can pretty much buy anything a person wants
if they have enough of it. It is certainly not a sin to be
rich, nor is it a sin to work very hard in an attempt
to be successful and have the finer things in life. It
is quite wrong though if one goes around with the
notion that their riches come from other than the
hand of God. All gifts come from God—PERIOD!
Whether it be monetary gifts, or gifts of athletic
ability, or gifts of math ability, or gifts of language
ability—all gifts come from God. "Those who trust
in themselves are foolish, but he who walks wisely
will be delivered" (Prov. 28:26). One need never feel
guilty about the gifts they have, instead, we must be
grateful for them and enjoy them. But it is what a
person does with those gifts that really matters, and

who gets credit for those gifts that really matters. So too, we must never complain about what we do not have, and we must not be jealous of others' gifts.

Over and over in the Bible, we read that God does not like a boastful heart, one that is puffed up, one that thinks it is something they did that has made them rich. We must remember that no one person is more important than the other in the eyes and plan of God. St. Paul tells us that "the body is not a single part, but many....You are Christ's body and individually part of it. And each part is needed for the other part to work properly. And without even the smallest part, the whole will not function properly....As such, no part of the structure of a living body is passive, but each has a share in the function as well as in the life of the body. Jesus is in our midst to guide and lead us, but we must become a team to serve as Jesus taught us and as Jesus did. Each person on the team must play a part in being the loving presence of Jesus to others."

Mother Teresa accomplished phenomenal tasks but never gave credit to herself for as much as a piece of paper. She and her sisters started each day in prayer, not only asking for God's blessings that day, but thanking God for all of His gifts the day before. She prayed for courage and strength and food and a loving heart, she prayed for direction and guidance and the gift of hope, and she prayed for healing and sustenance. She never assumed but prayed with absolute confidence that she would be given all that she needed to continue her work. She never worried for she trusted totally in the grace of God to carry her. She never knew where she would go and what she was to do on any given day, but always felt directed and never felt lost. And at the end of each day, she thanked her God and acknowledged His absolute and total control over her life. She gave credit where credit was due, and she slept in the peace that God would give her and her sisters whatever they needed. "Therefore, I tell you, do not worry about your life, what you will eat or drink; or about your body, what you will wear….Look at the birds of the air; they do not sow or reap or store away in barns, and yet your heavenly Father feeds them. Are you not much more valuable than they? Who of you by worrying can add a single hour to his life. And why do you worry about clothes? See how the lilies of the field grow. They do not labor or spin. Yet I tell you that not even Solomon, in all his splendor, was dressed like one of these. If that is how God clothes the grass of the field, which is here today and tomorrow is thrown into the fire, will He not much more clothe you, Oh you of little faith? So do not worry, saying, 'What shall we eat?' or "What shall we drink?' or "What shall we wear?'…Therefore, do not worry about tomorrow" (Matt. 6: 25–28).

Mother Teresa never boasted about what she did, and was the absolute model of humility, knowing full well and believing totally that she would get her spiritual reward for her works of mercy. So too we must be on this earth, not seeking to brag about the good that we do, or the money that we give to the poor, or the time that we spend in helping others. Scripture tells us to "be careful not to do your 'acts of righteousness' before men, to be seen by them. If you do, you will have no reward from your Father in heaven. So when you give to the needy, do not announce it with trumpets, as the hypocrites do in the synagogues and on the streets, to be honored by men. I tell you the truth, they have already received their reward in full. But when you give to the needy, do not let your left hand know what your right hand is doing, so that your giving may be in secret. Then your Father, who sees what is done in secret, will reward you" (Matt. 6:1–4).

Dear good and gracious God!
Please give us the gifts of humility and wisdom—
Humility to accept the truth that
*   everything comes from you,*
And wisdom to never forget this truth.
We ask this all in the most holy name of
*   Jesus Christ, Your Son, Amen.*

Suffering

Then call on me in time of distress;
I will rescue you and you shall honor me.
—Psalm 50:15

"The biggest disease today is not leprosy or tuberculosis, but rather the feeling of being unwanted, uncared for and deserted by everybody" (Mother Teresa). One need not look very far to find suffering. It is within everyone's reach and within everyone's sight. It surrounds us on any given day and does not go away. It can be lessened for a while but, for many, it is a way of life, a way of survival. For many, its only relief may be death. It comes in so many forms—physical, emotional, psychological, spiritual. For some, it may wax and wane, but for many, it is always there forever. What is thrown away on any given day may be the difference between life and death to someone starving. There is personal suffering—our child gets arrested for drunk driving, our mother is diagnosed with cancer, our business goes bankrupt, our marriage ends in divorce. We many times feel we cannot go on and then somehow there appears the grace to continue. Suffering is many times a way that God uses to prune us, to give us a wake-up call, to strengthen our need for Him. It is a time that brings us to our knees and opens our eyes to those things which are really important. It is a time that we realize how much we have and changes our focus to recognizing what we have left as opposed to what we have lost. Mother Angelica tells us that "a diamond at one time was a piece of coal. By unbelievable pressure, this ugly piece of coal is turned into a diamond. It's sort of like our interior lives. A lot of us are inundated by pressures, all permitted by the Lord, intended to transform us into spiritual diamonds" (Arroyo 2007).

We many times blame God for our suffering—we make bad decisions in the stock market and lose our savings—how can God let this happen? We drink two cases of beer a day and lose our health or our marriage—why would a loving God allow this? We cheat on our wife and end up in divorce—how can our God do this to me? Yes, we suffer, but we are many times the cause of our own suffering—not God. "We all have crosses, and some we make ourselves. But all of us have a personal cross from God Himself, designed specifically for us. That cross, whether it is physical, mental, spiritual, whatever it is, that particular cross is the main reason why you will be holy and it indicates your glory in heaven. Your entire glory in heaven will be dependent on how you carried your cross" (Arroyo 2007).

Once we tame our suffering and recognize it for what it is, we can focus on decreasing the suffering of those around us, one person at a time. When we see someone suffering psychologically, listen to them, talk to them, do not avoid them, smile at them, try to understand them. If we see someone suffering physically, clothe them by buying them a jacket, feed them by buying them a sandwich—take action and don't just look at them and smile. Mother Angelica tells us, "When a poor person dies of hunger, it does not happen because God would not take care of him or her. It has happened because neither you nor I wanted to give that person what he or she needed." Recognize trials that are sent your way as something "sent to disable the mechanism or self-reliance that we create for ourselves" (Arroyo 2007). "Sin has a way of sticking to us.…That is the world: it stinks and it clings to you. Pretty soon, you don't smell it anymore. That's the way habitual sin, serious sin is. We cannot get in the Presence of God forever smelling like that. That is the purpose of suffering, to remove the smell!" (Arroyo 2007).

Do not look at suffering as a punishment from God or something given to you because of a lack of faith; look at it instead as God selecting you to suffer for His glory. Max Lucado tells us that "Your faith in the face of suffering cranks up the volume of God's song.…His light prisms through their aching lives and spills forth in a cascade of colors. God-glimpses" (Lucado 2004).

> *Dear good and gracious God!*
> *Let me recognize suffering in the lives of*
> *   others and do something about it.*
> *Let me look at those less fortunate*
> *   and see Your face.*
> *Let me use the suffering you send me*
> *   for Your greater glory.*

And let me forever recognize the
suffering You send me as the cross
You have sent me to bear,
On my way to Your glory.
We ask this in the most holy name of
Jesus Christ, Your Son, Amen.

Temptation

No temptation has seized you except
what is common to man.
And God is faithful; He will not let you be
tempted beyond what you can bear.
But when you are tempted,
He will also provide a way out so that
you can stand up under it.
—1 Corinthians 10:13

"We all begin by silencing our conscience, looking the other way, putting aside this principle or that. And one day, you look back and you have sold your soul for a peanut. Doesn't matter what it is—it's all peanuts compared to the value of your soul" (Arroyo 2007). The devil is the father of lies and is constantly trying to enslave us. In essence, he says to us constantly, "It's not *really* bad. How do you know you shouldn't do it? It won't *really* hurt anyone. Everyone else is doing it." He convincingly reels us in ever so subtly and suddenly we reach a point in our lives where we no longer feel guilt, we no longer feel remorse, we no longer have the ability to control our desires, and we have become slaves to ourselves. As mentioned before, "sin has a way of sticking to us…it stinks and clings to us. Pretty soon, you don't smell it anymore" (Arroyo 2007).

"You know, if you are bit by a chained dog, you can't blame the dog. If you put yourself in temptation and you fall, you cannot blame anyone but yourself. The devil has been chained, but when you go live in his pen, you are risking eternity. The grace…of Jesus has penned him up. But when you give your mind, and heart, and will over to temptation, the teeth marks are on your soul" (Arroyo 2007). The devil never tires of trying to lure you into following him. He attacks your weakest point and works on your vulnerability. He is sly and cunning and forever works on his strategy to trick you, to lure you, to weaken you, to capture you. We are constantly in a battle with him and he never tires. We must every day fight him off with all our might. We must surround ourselves with friends that help us in this battle and are there to correct us, to encourage us in our spiritual walk, to pray with us, to strengthen us. The devil's intent is to make us prisoners of ourselves and to convince us that we need not serve others. We must recognize our foes and defeat them. It is a constant struggle, but we can be made strong if we give our heart and soul to God, and every day recommit to do battle with temptation.

God never gives us more than He gives us the grace to handle if we but ask for His help. Pray always and clear your minds of evil thoughts and desires and temptations. Replace these with good thoughts and the desire to help others. Look down the rungs of the ladder instead of up and recognize all that you do have compared to what you do not have. Do not complain and be unhappy with your lives. Mother Teresa tells us that "the more you have, the more you are occupied, the less you give. But the less you have, the freer you are. Poverty for us is a freedom. It is not mortification, a penance. It is joyful freedom. There is no TV here, no this, no that. But we are joyfully happy." Speak out against evil, against injustice, against wrongdoing, against corruption, against sin, and recognize without a doubt that "the only thing needed for the triumph of evil is that good men do nothing" (Kreeft 1990). Love all and serve them.

"The liberating solution to all temptations is simplicity: not to **add** some new method or technique or idea but to **subtract**, to ignore everything except 'God said no, therefore I will not say yes.' Or 'God said yes so I will not say no.' Period. Simple love deals in periods" (Kreeft 1990, emphasis added). Listen to what God tells you and ignore everything else, simply and in total truth—PERIOD!

> *Dear good and gracious God!*
> *Give us Your strength and courage to*
> *be strong and courageous;*
> *To stand up for what we know to be true*
> *and reject what we know to be lies;*
> *To feel Your peace and presence about us,*
> *And to know that we can resist temptation*
> *as we ask for Your holy presence*
> *in our lives at all times.*
> *We ask this all in the most holy name of*
> *Jesus Christ, Your Son, Amen.*

Conclusion

For even the Son of Man came not
to be served but to serve,
And to give his life as a ransom for many.
—Mark 10:45

"When you look at electrical things, you can see that they are made of small and big wires, cheap and expensive all lined up. Until the current runs through them, there will be no light. Those wires are you and me, and the current is God. We have the power to let the current pass through us, use us, and produce the light of the world, or we can refuse to be used and allow darkness to spread" (Mother Teresa). And so we are now called to go out into the world and serve after first getting right with God and completely emptying ourselves of doing our will. We are called to pray and ask for God's blessings and for the gifts of the Holy Spirit so that we can recognize God's will in our lives and plan He has for us.

Let us be Christ to others—full of love and compassion and mercy. Let us not judge or ask why—let us merely serve our fellow man in any way we can without question, without reserve, without reward, without judgment. Let us journey on the long and narrow path that we know in our hearts we must travel to reach our ultimate goal in this, our earthly life. Let us know what we must do to travel that road and let us do so with courage and strength. Let us not be afraid, as Jesus tells us, to *get out of the boat* of comfort and venture out of our comfort zones onto the paths of those we are called to help, those we are called to serve, those we are called to complete, those we are called to help survive. And let us not be afraid to be called "slaves of Jesus Christ" as we journey through life helping one person at a time to reach dignity. Mother Teresa tells us, "If you can't feed a hundred people, then feed just one." Make a difference, no matter how small. "Let your light shine before men, that they may see your good deeds and glorify your Father who is in heaven" (Matt. 5:16).

Will you let me be your servant?
Let me be as Christ to you?
Pray that I may have the grace to,
Let you be my servant, too.
We are pilgrims on a journey,
We are travelers on the road;
We are here to help each other,
Walk the mile and bear the load.
I will hold the Christ-light for you,
In the nighttime of your fear;
I will hold my hand out to you,
Speak the peace you long to hear.
I will weep when you are weeping;
When you laugh, I'll laugh with you.
I will share your joy and sorrow.
Till we've seen this journey through.
When we sing to God in heaven,
We shall find such harmony,
Born of all we've known together,
Of Christ's love and agony.
Will you let me be your servant?
Let me be as Christ to you?
Pray that I may have the grace to,
Let me be your servant too.

References

Agar, Herbert. *A Declaration of Faith*. 1950. Boston. Houghton Mifflin Company.

Al-Anon Family Group Headquarters, Incorporated. *One Day at a Time in Al-Anon.* 1988.

Arroyo, Raymond. 2007. *Mother's Angelica's Little Book of Life Lessons and Everyday Spirituality*. New York: Doubleday.

Chambers, Oswald. 1963. *The Utmost for His Highest*. Uhrichsville: Barbour.

Johnston, Francis W. 1965. *The Voice of the Saints*. Rockford: Doubleday.

Kelly, Matthew. 2002. *Rediscovering Catholicism*. Cincinnati: Beacon.

Kelly, Matthew. 1999. *The Rhythm of Life*. Cincinnati: Beacon.

Kernfield, Jack. *A Path With Heart, a Guide Through the Perils and Promises of Spiritual Life.* 1974.

Kreeft, Peter. 1990. *Making Choices.* Ann Arbor: Servant Books.

Lucado, Max. 2004. *It's Not About Me.* Nashville: Integrity.

Reynolds, Luke. 2006. "Priests, Brothers and Sisters Enrich Others with God's Graces." *The Criterion*, Indianapolis: 28 July, 2006, 16.

Rinpoche, Sogyal. *The Tibetan Book of Living and Dying.* Harper Collins. 1992

Warren, Rick. *The Purpose-Driven Life.* 2008. Broadman and Holman.

Milton Keynes UK
Ingram Content Group UK Ltd.
UKHW010839080823
426516UK00001B/4

9 781643 450438